negative space

a memoir

lilly dancyger

20 YEARS *sf*WP)

sfwp.com

PRAISE FOR *Negative Space*

"Using images and text, *Negative Space* shows us the New York art scene of the 1980's and the author's late father—but neither are ghosts here. They are written with full splendor, tenderness, and possibility. Exploring her artistic legacy, Dancyger confronts what it means to create and build meaning from absence. Candid, thrilling, wickedly smart, *Negative Space* is one of the greatest memoirs of this, or any, time."

—T Kira Madden, author of *Long Live the Tribe of Fatherless Girls*

Negative Space is a lovely and heartbreaking book; navigating pain, inheritance, and loss. Dancyger's father emerges from these pages as vividly as if I'd known him.

—Carmen Maria Machado, author of *In the Dream House*

"This book is so many things: a daughter's heartrending tribute, a love story riddled by addiction, a mystery whose solution lies at the intersection of art and memory. Together, they form a chorus that I could not turn away from, and didn't wish to. Like all great works, like those of the author's father, this book resists description but articulates something profound—about grief, art, and love—that could not have been communicated in any other way."

—Melissa Febos, author of *Whip Smart* and *Abandon Me*

"Lilly Dancyger creates an unflinching account of her artist father's snakebitten life and his struggles with addiction – peeling back the layers around an artistic practice that seems weighted with vulnerability. Ultimately, he comes painfully alive as Dancyger charts an elegiac path to her own self-discovery."

—Cynthia Carr, author of *Fire in the Belly:
The Life and Times of David Wojnarowicz*

Negative Space is a brilliant, moving, unique, thought-provoking meditation on the artistic life, fathers and daughters, and the struggle to live life at the highest pitch in each generation. This is a rare book about art, and one to treasure.

—Mark Greif, author of *Against Everything*

"This fierce, intimate work explores the ways in which we construct identities for the people with whom we're closest, and how we must eventually look beyond those constructs in order to see the world the way it really is…"

—*Refinery 29*, Most Anticipated Books of 2021 List

"Dancyger dives deeply into the liminal space of grief and loss in order to re-collect traces of her father as well as pieces of self. As she travels the past picking up remnants and clues from her father's art and life, Lilly brings to form new stories of family and identity as their own works of art. *Negative Space* is a beautiful restoration act that brings her own art and heart to life."

—Lidia Yuknavitch, author of *The Chronology of Water*

"In *Negative Space*, Dancyger achieves that beautiful, often elusive, balance of writing about addiction with equal parts examination and empathy. Unraveling the missing facts about her father's life, addiction, and death, through memory, investigation, and his art, she writes with an eye to understanding that we are all more than one "thing," that parents are humans first and parents second, that people in the throes of addiction are multi-dimensional. As someone who struggled with heroin addiction for many years, as her father did, the care with which she told this story is exquisite. At turns heartbreaking, reflective, and light, I tore through this book and, when I was done, found myself returning to pages I had marked, passages I had underlined, because the story unfolds in layers, just like life does."

— Erin Khar, author of *Strung Out: One Last Hit and Other Lies that Nearly Killed Me*

"*Negative Space* is made of a daughter's love, a detective's quest, and a true wordsmith's gift of beautiful prose. Dancyger pursues the clues left behind by her father in the provocative, often disturbing artwork he made, clues not only to his mind but to the central mysteries of her life. Her story itself becomes provocative, harrowing--and deeply moving. This book is a true accomplishment, one that often left me stunned and disturbed in all the right ways, all the ways brilliant art does. In writing about her artist father, Dancyger has herself created a work of art."

—Alex Marzano-Lesnevich, author of *The Fact of a Body*

"Dancyger's memoir is a page turner, the details in this book stayed with me, I dare you to put it down."

—Sofia Perpetua, journalist, goodreads.com

Library of Congress Cataloging-in-Publication Data
Names: Dancyger, Lilly, author.
Title: Negative space / Lilly Dancyger.
Description: Santa Fe : Santa Fe Writers Project, 2021. | Summary: "Despite her parents' struggles with addiction, Lilly Dancyger always thought of her childhood as a happy one. But what happens when a journalist interrogates her own rosy memories to reveal the instability around the edges? Dancyger's father, Joe Schactman, was part of the iconic 1980s East Village art scene. He created provocative sculptures out of found materials like animal bones, human hair, and broken glass, and brought his young daughter into his gritty, iconoclastic world. She idolized him-despite the escalating heroin addiction that sometimes overshadowed his creative passion. When Schactman died suddenly, just as Dancyger was entering adolescence, she went into her own self-destructive spiral, raging against a world that had taken her father away. As an adult, Dancyger began to question the mythology she'd created about her father-the brilliant artist, struck down in his prime. Using his sculptures, paintings, and prints as a guide, Dancyger sought out the characters from his world who could help her decode the language of her father's work to find the truth of who he really was. A memoir from the editor of Burn It Down: Women Writing About Anger, Negative Space explores Dancyger's own anger, grief, and artistic inheritance as she sets out to illuminate the darkness her father hid from her, as well as her own"—Provided by publisher.
Identifiers: LCCN 2020027267 (print) | LCCN 2020027268 (ebook) | ISBN 9781951631031 (paperback) | ISBN 9781951631048 (ebook)
Subjects: LCSH: Dancyger, Lilly. | Adult children of drug addicts—United States—Biography. | Journalists—United States—Biography.
Classification: LCC HV5132 .D353 2021 (print) | LCC HV5132 (ebook) | DDC 362.29/14092 [B]—dc23
LC record available at https://lccn.loc.gov/2020027267
LC ebook record available at https://lccn.loc.gov/2020027268

Published by SFWP
369 Montezuma Ave. #350
Santa Fe, NM 87501
(505) 428-9045
www.sfwp.com

For my father, Joe Schactman.
And for everyone living with an absence.

Author's Note

To write this book, I relied on my own memory where applicable—as well as my father's notebooks and letters, my mother's journals, and over two dozen interviews. The stories I collected through these interviews often contradicted each other, and sometimes themselves. I did my best to find something like the truth in the in-between spaces where all of these various sources overlapped.

For a long time, I struggled with the presumptiveness of telling someone else's life story without their input—especially someone as proud and opinionated as my father. But the more I saw how rarely two people remembered the same event in the same way, the more I realized that even if I could have interviewed my father directly, I still wouldn't have gotten "the truth," whatever that even means. So this story is a truth—one of many.

Archival Note

All photographs of the artwork included here were taken by the author unless otherwise noted. Where locations are noted, pieces were photographed at the homes of friends and relatives who own them; where no location is noted, they are from the author's personal collection. Because records are scarce and incomplete, most pieces are untitled, and materials listed are the author's best guesses based on examination.

There's a photograph of my father laughing on the last day I saw him alive. It's in a two-part frame with a picture of me, also laughing, taken in the same moment. His hand is over his mouth, covered in nicks, cuts, and callouses from working with wood and concrete at his construction job and in his art studio. Our faces are both red from laughing until we were gasping for air.

I look at these photos and try to hear the sound. Sometimes I can remember his laugh, and sometimes when I try there's just silence. I can't remember what was so funny, either, but I remember how totally enraptured and entertained I was by him, and how proud to know that he felt the same about me.

It was Easter Sunday, 2000. I was eleven, almost twelve. I hadn't seen my father in half a year, and we were living on opposite sides of the country. My mother had brought me to San Francisco to spend the weekend with him.

At the end of that Sunday, the three of us had dinner at a '50s-style diner covered in chrome called Hamburger Mary's, on Folsom Street. Sitting in the red vinyl banquet, I had a grilled cheese and a chocolate milkshake, which I drank as slowly as possible to extend our visit by just a few more minutes. We all talked and laughed together so comfortably that I imagined I might finally get the wish I'd been holding onto for four years: that my parents might remember that they loved each other, and get back together.

When my milkshake was gone and it was time to go, I cried and held onto fistfuls of my father's shirt like I had when I first learned he wasn't going to be living with us anymore. I dug my nails into the flannel and breathed in the stale cigarette smoke and the faintly chemical plaster smell. He hugged me and let me cry, waiting for me to get it all out. But when I didn't stop, didn't let go, he finally took my hands in his, leaned his face in close to mine, and said, "I'm sorry, sweetheart. I have to go. I love you."

He wrote me a letter on his bus ride home. Starting with his signature self-deprecating humor, he wrote, "You somehow manage to look so much like my daughter (the Schactman family resemblance is very strong) + yet still you manage to be so beautiful."

He implored me not to let adolescence shrink me. "Stand up and be proud," he wrote, warning that young women sometimes hide their intelligence to avoid drawing attention to themselves. "Never be embarrassed by your ability to make just the right sentence, with all of the exact words you wanted and needed."

He praised my vocabulary and articulate speech, and drew a comparison between language and his use of images as an artist, which would become even more valuable to me once I grew up and built a life around words: "The more closely you look at something, the more likely it is that you'll be able to draw that something, and the more you draw, the better you see. Well, knowing how to use language accurately and well, and being able to take pleasure in it, means that your brain is always able to think more and more accurately and elegantly."

And he apologized for how his heroin addiction had affected me. He never referred explicitly to drugs, but, euphemistically, to "the stuff I've been going through." He'd recently been arrested and spent time in inpatient rehab; he could no longer hope I wouldn't notice. But he still couched it in gentle terms—to protect me, or his dignity, I'm not sure.

By the time that letter arrived, he was dead. Those last words of fatherly praise and advice became as precious as Moses' tablets; words from beyond, all there would ever be.

When my father died, I knew he was clean because he'd told me over the phone that he was healthy and doing really well, and I'd heard the lightness in his voice and known it was true. We'd made plans to camp under the redwoods in Northern California, and I knew his excitement wasn't just about this visit we were planning, but about his new start, finally off drugs. I knew, but all of the adults seemed to know just as surely that he'd died of an overdose. I could hear them whispering when they thought I wasn't paying attention, and I saw the way they looked at me, like I was about to get more bad news. I knew they thought I was in denial, that I couldn't understand such adult things.

We had the funeral without proof either way, still waiting for the medical examiner's report.

My father's friend Audrey had everyone over a couple of days before the funeral, to be together and mourn and drink and talk. I didn't like how everyone was looking at me, so I mostly hid in her bedroom, lying curled up like a cat on the pile of everyone's coats on the bed. I came out at one point, and as I stepped into the living room, I heard someone say in a loud whisper, "I mean, it had to be an overdose, right?"

I was entering the room from behind them, and they hadn't seen me yet. I very quietly sidled up to the couch, leaning in until my face was just a few inches from theirs and hissed, "It wasn't."

I'd hardly spoken at all in the first hazy days since his death, and my voice came out dry and brittle. Everyone in the room looked up, realizing what had happened, wondering if this was the moment my quiet shock would shatter into torrential, raging grief. They all stared at me, waiting.

I fled back into the bedroom to burrow into the pile of coats and cry, as much from anger as from grief. There was a collective sigh that said they still didn't believe me.

The autopsy report came days or weeks later, confirming that there was no heroin in my father's blood when he died. My mother clutched it in both hands as she said the words, "It wasn't an overdose." I collapsed, sobbing with both of my palms and my forehead pressed into the floor like a child's pose in yoga, letting go of the weight of being the only one to defend him. Her breath was shaking as she pulled me up and into her arms, still holding the report tight in her fist, smudging it with her sweat and strain and relief. She'd been clean herself for four years by then, and I knew she wanted as badly as I did to believe that he hadn't been taken down by the monster that had chased them both for so long. But she also knew better than I did how easily it could have come back for him, even after he thought he'd escaped it.

The coroner couldn't determine a clear cause of death, which left us with so many questions—they said it seemed like he vomited while sleeping on his back and choked, but they couldn't be sure enough to list that as the official cause. They tested each of his organs. They saved some of his tissue in case future tests became available that might tell us which switch flipped and made my father's body stop living at 43 years old. My mother couldn't stop speculating, and still does sometimes— wondering if he died of long-term lead poisoning from using the toxic metal in his sculptures, or even if the women whose farm he was living on while he did a big construction job for them had poisoned him so they wouldn't have to pay the money they owed.

But it didn't really matter to me how he died, as long as it wasn't drugs. I didn't know at twelve years old that overdose isn't the only way drugs can kill you, and took the report from the coroner as proof that my father's death was unrelated to his problem—that, as I understood it then, it wasn't his fault. It was a victory I held tightly for years. "Undetermined causes" became a phrase I returned to, a reminder that bad things just happen sometimes. I took a strange kind of comfort in the fact that my father's death had no explanation, as slippery and maddening a fact as it was.

In preparation for the funeral, my mother and aunt took me shopping for black clothing. I floated through the racks at Macy's like my feet were hovering above the ground. When we went shopping before the start of each new school year, I was giddy, running around and collecting armfuls of trendy polyester hideousness. I grabbed and grabbed until I had a pile as big as me, imagining a whole new wardrobe. Then my mother and I would whittle that pile down to a couple of new things: a pair of jeans on sale, one new dress. Treasures.

But this time I barely noticed where I was. The brightness of the pastel shirts with their big plastic daisies and over-bold patterns faded into the background as I slowly and quietly picked out one simple knee-length dress for the service, and a few black shirts and skirts to wear for an as-yet-undetermined mourning period. I wanted to make it visibly clear that I was not fully present, not available for normal human interaction; that my entire being was busy grieving. I understood then the long history of mourning rituals: shaving your head, tearing your clothes, periods of total seclusion. I thought of the "FRAGILE" stickers we pasted on the boxes of my father's artwork—I wanted the clothing version. A warning: *Handle with care.* But while I wanted my mourning to be visible, I also wanted to disappear. So instead of black lace veils and a bald head, I hid inside of plain black t-shirts from the juniors' department for the rest of middle school.

Less than a month after my father died and a week before I started seventh grade, my mother and I moved across the country for the third of four times, to California's Central Coast.

We moved there for her to get back together with the man she'd first started dating right after she and my father broke up, an engineer named Tom. He was big and tall and quiet and he had long, long hair and long, long fingers. He didn't have any kids, and he didn't know how to interact with me at seven when they got together the first time, let alone at twelve, grieving and more resentful than ever. He wanted his hot girlfriend and he got her sad, angry kid, too. Raw deal for both of us.

Tom worked for the Army Corps of Engineers, and was living in the housing they provided in Fort Ord—an old military base converted into a suburb in Monterey County. We moved in with him on a cul-de-sac of identical two-story apartment houses, white stucco on the outside and all beige on the inside. The cul-de-sac was connected by the main road to about a dozen other identical cul-de-sacs populated with identical two-story apartment houses. The spaces between the cul-de-sacs were thick woods. There wasn't a store or restaurant within walking distance—or even on the base. My mother didn't have a car, so I only ever left that maze of desolate suburbia on the school bus that took me to a middle school where I was not only the new kid from across the country, but the new kid from across the country still blinking in the shell shock of fresh grief, which looked, to my fellow middle schoolers, like shy awkwardness. They looked like nothing to me. I can't remember any of their faces or names—except for one girl, Emily, who I made friends with because she brought fake blood to school and dribbled it from her mouth to make people think she was dying. I liked her.

Fort Ord hadn't been an active military base in years but had only recently been converted into this sprawling, bleak housing complex. It retained the eerie quiet of abandoned space. I'd occasionally see a car drive by, but I don't remember ever seeing anyone walking on the clean, uniform sidewalks. It was almost like my mind had projected this place. This was what the world looked like without my father in it: monotonous and hollow. And I changed to match that world. I spoke as little as possible. I avoided moving my face from the blank, heavy expression it would wear if I were to hang it up on a wall like a rubber mask, sagging. Any movement from that position could easily have been derailed into crying.

There was a playground on Fort Ord, right behind our house. Tom's house. I never saw any kids there. I remember walking down the driveway, out of the cul-de-sac, onto the main road, and into the playground to sit on a swing. I didn't swing enough that my feet left the ground, just rocked almost imperceptibly back and forth. I hadn't brought my Discman or a book, so I just stared straight ahead at two crows pacing around on the grass and the tall trees with strips of bark peeling off, their branches swaying as softly as I was swinging. When I think of that time, that's the image that comes to mind: me, sitting on a nearly-still swing, in an empty playground, on an abandoned military base, under a heavy sky that was solid white like it was always about to rain. It was like *The Wizard of Oz* in reverse—like I'd been in a world of color, and then a twister hit and dropped me into black and white.

My mother watched me descend into numbness and reached out to pull me back. She watched, waiting for me to scream and sob and break things. But I didn't. I had done all of those things when I first learned my father was dead—thrown plates and empty flower pots out of our second-story window and watched them shatter in the alley below, screamed and pounded the floor with my fists. And then I'd gone quiet. I was always on the verge of tears but didn't cry, like the heavy white sky that never broke open and rained.

In a stroke of maternal ingenuity, my mother proposed that we share a journal where we could write letters to each other.

"I know that it can be hard for you to talk," she wrote on the first page, "and maybe this will help you to not have to hold on to everything all by yourself."

In an entry dated seven weeks after my father died, I made a timid attempt to use the journal, coming out of hiding in slow motion like a starving kitten: "I was just thinking and decided to tell you what about, since that is what this is for," I wrote. "I want to tell you that when I am at school every now and then for a few minutes, it takes all of the self-control I have to keep from bursting into tears. I will suddenly realize that now Papa is not only on the other side of the country."

This simple confession barely scratched the surface, but it was a huge step. The emotion was too large, I didn't know what to do with it, so my adolescent response was to feel embarrassed by how much I hurt. Embarrassed by how undone I felt by grief, and unaccustomed to sharing anything vulnerable with my mother, my cheeks burned as I wrote this plainest possible admission.

Her excitement that I was willing to communicate with her at all, her eagerness to connect, to share, to help, possessed her and erased any sense of delicacy she may have had. Her response started with her wish to protect me, "I can't stand it," she wrote. "I wish I wish I wish."

After a paragraph about that, she turned to her own pain, to an expression of it so naked I had no idea what to make of it. She gushed about how much she loved my father, how she wanted me to know that even though things weren't always good with them, she'd loved him more than anyone in the world except for me; how they shared a "hard fierce intense deep passionate real true love," and how she hoped I'd have a love like that someday. She described sitting in the apartment alone, listening to The Replacements and crying. The entry became about their love, which I had watched rot and turn into screaming hatred just a few years before, the biggest heartbreak of my life until his death. Her response to my tiny step out into the open was such a torrent of emotion, so many confessions and so much intensity, I felt drowned in it.

I wrote a few more entries in the diary—one about a boy at school I'd convinced myself to develop a crush on, and a few about how much I hated Tom—but not one of them mentioned my father or my grief again.

When we first got to Fort Ord and were unpacking our things in Tom's apartment, we came across the big cardboard box full of my father's notebooks.

"Do you think we should read them?" my mother asked, trying to sound casual, as if it wasn't a huge question. I gaped at her while she waited, her hand still on the flap of the box, the question still on her face. We were sitting on the beige carpet of the long hallway, surrounded by boxes. She was wearing cotton pajama pants and one of Tom's t-shirts, her hair dyed black with red highlights that flashed like embers when the sun hit them, tied into a tight, high ponytail. She wasn't wearing makeup, and she looked tired, but hopeful.

I thought of my own sticker-covered journals, full of preteen confessions of hopeless crushes and self-loathing. The possibility of someone reading them when I died instilled in me a fear of my own mortality unlike any I'd felt before. I couldn't subject my father to that indignity, and I wanted to set a clear precedent that dead people's privacy was not to be invaded—just in case.

I finally managed to get out a "No!" and then after a few more long seconds, "No, we definitely should not do that." She acquiesced and closed the box, which we moved, unopened, from apartment to apartment for the next eight years. We moved his notebooks, his sculptures and prints and drawings and paintings, his leather jacket, his books, every scrap of paper he had ever scribbled on, and every photo ever taken of him. Boxes and boxes of ephemera crowding the corners of each small apartment we lived in, surrounding us, replacing his bodily presence. Anchoring his memory with things.

They say all the cells in your body regenerate every seven years. When I turned twenty, my father had been dead for eight—so if that theory is true, no cell in my body had ever been on the planet at the same time as him. I'd changed, cell by cell, into a person he never knew.

I was in college, learning new things that I couldn't debate with him or get his opinion on, that I had to decide the value of for myself. I had an apartment in the East Village with a roommate I loved like a sister, whom he'd never met. I was bartending, part of my neighborhood community not as the daughter of a local artist, but as myself. I had a whole life, and my father wasn't in it. With every step forward, I was acutely aware that I was moving further and further from the version of me that had known him, or even a version of me that he would recognize.

I was entering the world as a fatherless woman after years as a fatherless girl, and I didn't know how to move forward without leaving my father behind. For all of my adolescence, I'd stayed rooted in my grief because that was where I'd felt most connected to him. It was where he had left me, like when I was little and my parents warned that if we ever got separated on the subway, I was to get out at the next stop and wait for them there. If I stayed in my grief, my father would know where to find me. But if I just went ahead and enjoyed college and started planning for a career and becoming my own full person in the world, leaving the heaviness of grief behind,

I feared then my father would be truly gone—somehow even more than he already was.

The only way to stop that from happening, I thought, was to find a new way to grieve for him. I needed my relationship with my father to change and grow, like every parent-child relationship changes when the child becomes an adult—even if that just meant my relationship with his absence.

I realized then that I'd been saving his notebooks, that subconsciously I'd always thought of them as one more letter from him, like the one that arrived days after he died. I'd been keeping this last little bit of him for a future when I would really need it. And I needed it now. A little bit of him that could be new to me, that I could discover with wonder. A way to bring my relationship with him into the present of my life; learning to see him in a new way so that I could mourn him in a new way.

That last letter he wrote on the bus was the fatherly advice that I rationed through my adolescence. I stretched it out and applied it to everything, telling myself over and over to "stand up and be proud," trying to hear it in his voice. Now I was on another precipice, looking toward adulthood, and I needed a new pearl of his wisdom. Just one more. One more letter from him that magically made it across the border of death, and I'd be able to step forward into the rest of my life.

I waited for an evening I knew my roommate Leah would be out, so I could have our tiny apartment to myself for this ritual. I didn't know what to expect, how overwhelmed or immersed I would be, and I didn't want to be interrupted. I thought about it for days ahead of time; while I sat in my literature and philosophy classes at the New School, while I poured drinks at Sidewalk Cafe, while Leah and I chain-smoked on our rickety fire escape late at night. I told Leah I was planning to read my father's notebooks for the first time, not expecting her to really understand what that meant but needing to tell someone.

"Woof," she said, flipping waves of fluffy auburn curls over her shoulder and taking a drag of her cigarette. It was somehow just the right reaction—better than if she'd offered encouragement or warning or asked questions. Just an acknowledgement that it was a heavy task.

I built myself up until finally I had an evening alone, no homework that absolutely had to be done that night, no bar shift to rush off to, and the courage built up to invade the privacy of a dead man. I poured myself a mug of cheap red wine and dug the box out of the back of my closet—the same cardboard box the notebooks had been in since my father died, battered and worn now, with "JOE - NOTEBOOKS" written on one side in Sharpie, in my mother's handwriting. I'd taken the box with me when I moved out, insistent that these records of my father's mind were mine to inherit. My vague promise of answers, my grief to carry.

I sat on the small patch of floor under my loft bed, the only space in my room, and took a deep breath before carefully unfolding the flaps of the box. There they were, my father's notebooks—handmade, with cardboard covers of various shapes and sizes, stitched together with thick, black, waxed thread, splattered with ink and paint and plaster. There were about a dozen of them. As I picked them up one by one, spreading them out on the floor around me, I smelled a waft of my father—like wet flannel, drying paint, and loose tobacco. Or was it just the dust, and memory?

None of the notebooks had dates on the covers or anything to indicate an order, and I didn't know where to start. I just sat there for a while, with all of them fanned out in front of me, before taking a big gulp of wine and picking one like a card out of a tarot deck. I grabbed one of the bigger notebooks, its corrugated cardboard cover flattened and softened with time. I ran my fingers over what was left of the grooves, feeling for traces of my father's hands.

The first page I opened to was full of notes for a sculpture; thoughts on how best to position an arm reaching toward the sky, with drawings of possible options and questions like, "Which kind of wire would be best to support the fingers?"

The next page, careful accounts of the progress of various pieces: "The titanium wire is absurd. Far too fragile—like trying to work with a pubic hair," and how he felt about each piece as it developed:

> clay/glue #1—I've no faith in this piece as it is. None—it's bad. I do hold the basic premise, the idea derived from the Japanese sticks, to be of value tho
>
> Glue/clay #2—figure w/ falling birds—looks good. An odd piece—I've not done anything quite like this before—if the red wire didn't work as nicely as it does w/ the skin as light-event I'd feel differently about it

I wasn't surprised to find notes for his work, but I flipped past them, looking for his thoughts on life, records of conversations and insecurities, something that felt like a letter. I flipped through notebook after notebook, rushing through hundreds of ideas and sketches for sculptures and prints.

Scrawled in black ink, his words spiraled around the page, changing direction with each new thought rather than marching in uniform rows. It was like he knew someone would read these pages one day, and had made them as inscrutable as possible. I turned the notebooks around and around as I tried to follow his thoughts, searching for a message.

On one page, he referred to a series of sculptures of flightless angels with concrete wings as "(self)-frustrate-ing/ed." I smiled at the fact that even his simple notes to himself had layered meaning. I remembered these sculptures—he'd made them not long after my parents split up, when he was struggling to get clean. He'd made clay molds using feathers he'd collected and poured concrete into them to make the wings, heavy and gray in contrast with the figures' clear silicone bodies, straining toward the sky. The potential to fly, thwarted.

I loved reading his words, his phrasing, seeing his curiosity and excitement, and trying to match the notes to pieces I remembered. Even his idiosyncratic spelling and punctuation were comforting, so many superfluous hyphens from the man who taught me so young that it's "by accident" or "accidentally"—never "on accident," and not to say "like" so much; a stickler for my proper use of language, but deciding for himself how things were spelled.

But I wanted so much more. I wanted my father to rise from these pages like an apparition. I wanted a trove of secrets. I wanted everything he'd kept from me when I was a child. He mentioned "the stuff I've been going through" in that last letter, but what was he going through, exactly? What was it like for him to try so hard to get clean, and to see his young daughter watching, alternately hopeful and disappointed, as he failed over and over? I wanted the rest of that story. I was ready now; he could tell me.

And I wanted advice. He always said how proud he was of me, but he was also careful not to push me too hard in any one direction. He gave me the lattice to grow on and left me to do the climbing myself. But what did he really hope for me? At the very least, I wanted a list of his favorite books. Something, anything that would leave me feeling like I knew him a little better. Just a little more of him, left behind for me.

When the notebooks were sitting in my closet, cloaked in a layer of dust, they were a promise of closure to come. But then I opened the treasure chest and a moth flew out. These were not transcripts of my father's inner life. There was no response here to the one-sided conversation I'd been having with him in my mind since he died. They were all about his work.

I sat there for hours, reading his barely legible notes. At first, I read each page carefully, following the curling path of his writing, squinting at words I couldn't quite make out. But after the second notebook, and the third, I started to get frantic as I realized that my father wasn't in these pages. I started to flip through them faster, one after another, almost cursing him.

Finally, I spotted my name in a paragraph, written sideways on the page in a short note about taking the Greyhound bus from San Francisco three hours down the coast to Carmel to visit me after my mother moved us there when I was nine, about a year after my parents broke up. He described sitting in a park waiting for me, "on the verge of tears thinking of her and her mother live-ing there, how nice, but expensive/white it is, but how great for Lilly," and the "middle-aged, upper-class white people, their cars, their shops, their town. The incongruity of me there."

I wanted to tell him that I felt just as out of place in Carmel as he did that day, that I knew it was too rich and fancy for us—poor people who made art and, until then, had lived in the East Village, Bushwick, Williamsburg, and the Mission District. I'd only ever lived in walk-up apartment buildings and taken public transportation, and was used to hearing as much Spanish spoken on the street as English. And then my mother moved us to a quaint, manicured little California beach town dripping with money and kitsch, and I couldn't sleep at night. The big house in Carmel that we moved into with Tom soon after they started dating the first time felt like a vast and crawling cave when the lights were out. There were no city noises outside, no noises at all other than the wind in the big sycamore tree out front, and the skittering of raccoon feet on the roof.

The last line of the entry caught in my throat and stung my eyes:

"Lilly is the thing that keeps surrealism in its most oppressive modes and pointlessness @ bay."

I wanted to tell him that he was *the* thing for me, too, during those years; the thing that kept me connected to anything familiar, that made me feel like I still belonged somewhere, even if it wasn't where I was. That his weekly art postcards felt like a literal lifeline, and I read each one over and over and hung them all on the wall above my bed to replicate the feeling of him sitting in a chair next to me until I fell asleep. I read the books he sent and imagined his voice reading them to me. I wanted to tell him that I didn't forget him when we left the city, that I never betrayed him by letting Carmel feel like home. I was as difficult for my mother and Tom to deal with as I could be, because to skip off into the Pacific Coast sunset with them would have been to accept this new life, without my father. There's a reason children feel the deep need to inform stepparents they're not their "real" parents as often as possible: it's not just anger, it's fear of abandoning the parent who's not there by forming a new family without them. Of passing on the feeling of betrayal that we feel so deeply ourselves.

I read that note and was flooded with memories of Carmel, of being so young and missing my father so much. I realized that even when he was still alive, long before my life outstripped his by so many years—when he was just a couple of hours up the coast and still sending me letters and books all the time, talking on the phone in the evenings after I'd done my homework—I'd already felt like I was leaving him behind. I saw all the layers of my loss at once, realizing that I'd lost him over and over again already and I was still losing him more now, and then I was clutching the notebook to my chest and sobbing hot tears and gasping breaths.

I had to face the fact that I'd done exactly what I'd been trying to avoid for so long: I'd entered a whole new life that my father was absent from, and that was never going to change. The notebooks hadn't given me more of him, they'd just reminded me that he was gone, and he would never be any less gone.

My childhood started in New York City and then ping-ponged back and forth across the country until my mother and I finally came back to the East Village the summer before I started high school. As soon as my Converse touched the sun-scorched sidewalk, I grew deep, stubborn roots. New York was home; it was where I had learned to walk on the cracked sidewalks, and where all of my earliest memories were formed. In the first few years of my life, my heartbeat and breath had aligned themselves to the rhythm of New York so that nowhere else ever felt right.

When we moved back, I felt like I was finally returning, as if from a long war. But I also felt like I was starting over, with no friends, no routines, nothing familiar or grounding. Both were true. I was in the strange position of coming home to somewhere unfamiliar.

That first summer, my mother and I stayed in the back room of my godmother Hannah's vintage store on Ludlow Street, sharing a loft bed high above her racks of inventory. At night, we slept next to each other, sweaty in the July heat, breathing in the smells of old fabric. During the day, my mother tried to find work and an apartment, and I walked around the old-and-new neighborhood, trying to make up for seven years of absence. I traced and retraced routes between the three nearest subway stations, the park, the river, the corner stores and diners. I memorized subway lines and my coffee order, fast-forwarding familiarity. I sat on the same bench in Tompkins Square Park every day until it felt like mine. Pacing the neighborhood, scenting it like a cat, I felt equal parts a vast, quenching relief and an aching, hollow sadness. I was home, but even at home I floated around the edges, slightly removed.

Because of the way youth stretches time, I felt like my father's death two years earlier had been long enough ago that I wasn't allowed to let it be a central part of my life anymore. It had been two whole grades ago, two cross-country moves ago, starting-to-wear-a-bra ago. Another life. It was something horrible that had happened in my childhood, but I was fourteen now and it was time to grow up and move on.

When I look back now, it's clear that two years is nothing, a flash, in the scope of life-altering, world-shattering grief. I hadn't even started to pick up the pieces yet; I'd just grown accustomed to living in fragments. But I didn't know that then, so I didn't understand why I still heard a constant, low ringing in my ears, why I'd never quite gotten my appetite back, why everywhere I was, even finally back home in New York, life looked like a movie playing in a dark room.

Memories of my father were everywhere. I'd lived in Buffalo when he died, where he'd visited just once, for a weekend. Then we moved to Fort Ord, blank and empty and unlike anywhere I could imagine my father. This was the first time since his death that I'd lived in a place where I remembered him. I walked into Tompkins and I could see him so clearly, sitting on a bench in the playground with a book, looking up after each page and squinting into the sun to make sure I was still there. I went to our favorite Polish diner and ordered fried potato pierogis with sour cream and apple sauce, and half expected his chicken schnitzel dinner with kasha and mushroom gravy to arrive at the table too. I went to the Met and stood in front of Madame X, the Sargent painting he had sent me multiple postcards of and pleaded with me to draw my version of for him, and let the tears roll down my cheeks without wiping them away, tourists giving me a wide berth.

He was everywhere here, but he wasn't. My return to the home we'd shared, a return home that should have also been a return to him, made his absence more immediate and tangible than ever. I was so relieved to be back, but I also felt a gnawing guilt for making new memories here without him.

When school started, I was too full of the excitement and dread of my bittersweet homecoming, the fascination and melancholy of finding my new place in the old neighborhood, to sit in drab classrooms all day and then go home and do busy-work assignments for hours.

I was part of the second class ever at Bard High School Early College, an accelerated program where students finish high school requirements in the first two years and then start college classes, graduating high school with an Associate's Degree. It was a good idea in theory, but finishing high school in two years required a massive amount of homework, which I couldn't be bothered to do. I had just discovered ABC No Rio, the punk-art community center around the corner from our new apartment, and I wanted to spend all of my time there—taking silk screening classes during the day and thrashing my body around at shows at night; drinking forties in the back garden and making out with strangers who were way too old for me, telling them I was sixteen. I was making friends with the weirdos in Tompkins, and I couldn't wait all day long to go sit in the dirty grass and plug myself into the culture I'd been deprived of for so long. There were still streets in the neighborhood I hadn't walked down since we got back, old favorite foods I hadn't eaten, music venues and galleries and indie theaters I hadn't explored. I felt like I'd just woken up from a coma, and had years' worth of life to make up for.

I went to school just often enough to make friends to skip class with. I quickly bonded with Rakhel, a tiny Jewish Satanist who knew all the words to Leftöver Crack's "Atheist Anthem," and Raiona, who I met on the first day and liked immediately, which had never happened at any other school I'd ever attended. We staked out a corner of the schoolyard where we smoked cigarettes and sang Janis Joplin and the Ramones. We hung out in the park, where we met Haley and Jael, fuck-ups from another high school in the neighborhood, and then the five of us were inseparable. We held hands and sang songs walking across the bridge to go to house shows in Williamsburg, and traded the cheap silver rings we all wore tons of, so that we could all carry pieces of each other with us always. We drew each other's portraits and read each other's tarot cards and pierced each other's ears and faces with safety pins. We told each other the secrets we'd each been carrying around, alone; I told them stories about my father. I'd found other kids who were smart and weird and loved to read but didn't care about school, and I knew for sure that New York was where I should have been all along.

One day when I actually made an appearance in class, my science teacher, an evil toad of a woman, was droning on about speciation or cell structure or some other interesting topic that she managed to make tedious beyond belief. I was so bored I could barely hear what she was saying. The only thing I was fully aware of was how bright and inviting the sunny day outside looked. From my seat, I could see a sliver of the East River, the light bouncing off the water so brilliantly I almost forgot how murky and disgusting it was. In the distance, I heard the Mister Softee ice-cream truck song and children laughing and screaming. The world outside was a caricature of exuberance, and the desire to just get up and walk out into it was so strong I could feel it pushing out of my chest and up my throat. I dug my nails into the already chipped and scribbled-on desk and tried to keep from screaming.

I was so absorbed in my desire to be elsewhere that I didn't notice Ms. Gamper sidle up next to me until I smelled her notorious halitosis and heard her ask snidely if I was paying attention, pleased with herself for busting me. Whether or not she knew I was ignoring her was so far beyond my concern that the moment felt surreal. I looked up at her, then back out the window at East River Park where I knew the squatters from Avenue C were sitting in the sun drinking forties, where I could join them within five minutes if I left now, and answered honestly, "No, I'm not."

I stood up, shoving my notebook full of doodles into my messenger bag next to my Discman and the pint of vodka I'd been saving for lunch, and walked out. Ms. Gamper called after me with some irrelevant threats about grades or detention, but I wasn't listening. I walked down the empty third-floor hallway, ran down the three flights of caged-in stairs, and waved goodbye to the security guard with a smile on my way out the front door. The second I stepped outside, it was like a flying dream. When I fly in dreams, I don't soar; I take huge bounds, where each step propels me high into the air and yards forward before I float slowly back down and then bounce upward again with the next step. Walking out of high school felt like that—the buoyancy of freedom. I never went back, my high school career over after one semester of ninth grade.

I knew I wouldn't be able to make it four whole years in that place, so I figured I might as well cut my losses early. And besides, my father had been a drop-out, and he was the smartest person I'd ever known. He always explained proudly that he'd dropped out of college because "art school kills the artist," that it was more important to learn to think for yourself than it was to meet arbitrary external requirements. He believed he was better off drawing things as he saw them rather than as they were taught, inventing his own techniques, learning about how materials behaved by experimenting with them rather than reading about them. I decided I would educate myself, like my father had. I had plenty of books to read, and there were art and dance classes I could take all over the city. My mother, exasperated, warned that she wasn't going to pay for whatever "random bullshit" classes I wanted to take when I was supposed to be in school for free. But that was fine. I got a job waiting tables at the little restaurant on our block that served exclusively grilled cheese sandwiches (it was called The Grilled Cheese), the always-stoned owner charmed and amused by the fourteen-year-old with a nose piercing and a hangover who insisted she'd make a great waitress.

I'd been thinking about dropping out practically since school started, but that day in Ms. Gamper's class, as I stared at the perfect sunny day outside, I realized there was nothing holding me back, really. There were rules I was "supposed to" follow, sure, but what would happen if I just…didn't?

"I refuse to let my schooling get in the way of my education" became my mantra. I knew that most people read Mark Twain in high school, but I thought it was much more fitting that I first heard that quote from a drunk in the park. I held a firm conviction that the bars on the windows of Bard's classrooms were a metaphor for the intellectual prison of the school system, designed to keep young minds from discovering any "real truths." I had clearly inherited my father's bravado and sense of intellectual superiority.

I've always wondered whether I would've dropped out if he had been alive. He'd been dead for almost three years by then, but if anyone had a prayer of convincing me to stay in school, it would have been him. Yes, he was a drop-out, but he was also the son of a professor, and had some surprisingly traditional values for an iconoclastic artist. I'm sure he would have wanted me to stay in school. But if he had tried to guilt me into it like he was so good at doing, I could have reminded him that he was a drop-out, too, quoted his own words back at him.

My mother was so powerless to stop me that I barely remember her objecting. I know she did, but I didn't register anything she said back then; she was a mute blur in my peripheral vision as the thrill of finally finding somewhere I belonged mixed with the still-buzzing thrum of grief, spinning into a kind of laugh-crying mania. Once in a while she tried to put her foot down and tell me I had to be home by a certain hour or I had to go to class or I couldn't stay over at random people's apartments without telling her where I was, or even the bare minimum demand that I still refused to comply with just because it was a demand: that I had to answer my cell phone when she called so she knew I was alive. She was inconsistent in her attempts at setting rules, and I knew she had nothing to back them up with, so I made a point of showing her that she had no power over me.

Once, my mother stood at the kitchen counter, which was actually a big piece of particle board laid flat on a pile of boxes of her sewing supplies that there was no space for in our one-room studio apartment, her hands shaking as she poured a bottle of Guinness into a glass. I was on my way out, and she asked where I was going. In the refrain of teenagers everywhere, I answered curtly, "Out."

She sighed the big heaving sigh of a mother at the end of her patience, and said, more to her beer than to me, "If you don't cut this shit out I'm not gonna have any choice but to send you to boarding school. Military school. Something."

When I didn't respond she finally looked up from her glass and met my gaze. I was standing at the door, my hand on the knob, staring her down, calling her bluff. Her shaking voice, and the fact that she'd faltered over boarding school or military school, made it abundantly clear that this was an empty threat. She was grasping for a last card to force me to fall in line, but she had nothing. The longer we held eye contact, the more I felt myself hardening against her. I took her in: her hair dyed bright red now and cut to her chin, with bangs; the short denim skirt that she'd sewed herself out of an old pair of men's jeans, a Motörhead shirt. She looked more like another teenager than like a teenager's mother. There were tears welling up in her eyes, desperation on her face. She looked weak, and I despised her for it. When she broke and looked down, her complete powerlessness and cluelessness about how to handle me written all over her face, I laughed. There was a small, quiet part of me that felt bad, but I smothered it.

"Oh yeah?" I asked. "And how exactly do you plan to pay for that?" She started crying, her frustration spilling out, her reserves tapped. And I gave her my best, practiced look of disdain, turning back on my way out the door to say, "Don't wait up."

After that, it was over. We both knew there was nothing she could do, and she stopped trying. Once in a while, when I was gone for days at a time, she'd ask, "Where the fuck were you?" and I'd just laugh and ask why the fuck she cared, and that would be that.

I was exuberant with the freedom I'd found, the friends I'd made, the neighborhood where I felt at home for the first time since the blurry memories of early childhood, but just under the surface was a depression that felt like panic. I felt everything, all at once. So I drank and got high so it made sense for me to laugh hysterically until tears ran down my cheeks and then sob until I was red in the face and choking. That turning point between laughter and tears was where I lived all the time, and inebriation was a convenient excuse to let it out.

I looked more or less how you might expect the delinquent child of East Village junkie artists to look: waist-length, stringy curls, dyed purple but faded and dingy; enough black eyeliner to be an extra in *The Crow*; teeny-tiny miniskirts I made out of scraps of fabric leftover from my mother's sewing projects, cut precisely so they were long enough to cover my ass but not an inch longer; ripped-up fishnets and steel-toed boots. A cigarette always in my hand and a perpetual "the fuck you lookin' at?" expression on my face. I weighed 95 pounds but was still formidable in a fight, all my rage and sadness exploding out of my tiny fists, heavy with silver rings. All the toughness of a fragile thing.

I spent my days running around the neighborhood, chugging Georgi vodka out of plastic water bottles and fantasizing about the apocalypse. My outlook revolved around the fact that I didn't plan to live past my twenties, so it didn't matter if the drugs I did were cut with all kinds of toxic shit, or if a fifteen-year-old girl really shouldn't walk alone on Avenue D at three in the morning. I smoked cigarettes not in spite of the fact that they'd shorten my life, but hoping they would. I had daily conversations with a homeless guy in the park called Swill, and sometimes when I bought a pint of Wild Irish Rose (aka "bum wine") for $2.40 with the obviously fake ID I'd chalked myself, I picked up an extra one for him and we drank them together out of brown paper bags while talking baby-talk to his dog, Jitters, and laughing about how fucked up the world was.

The only days I didn't start drinking first thing were the days I took ballet classes at the Third Street Music School or Joffrey. I strained against structure everywhere else, but in the studio, I found it calming. I tied my badly-dyed hair back in a bun and wiped off my eyeliner, wore the same plain pink tights as everyone else, and almost blended in. For ninety minutes at a time, as sweat shone on my skin and my muscles stretched and strengthened, my breath filled my ribcage rather than fluttering shallow in my throat. My mind stopped racing, emptied of everything other than the hypnotizing "*one* two three four, *one* two three four" rhythm and the feeling of the rubber-mat floor under my feet. After class, I'd rush out to the park to quench my dancer's thirst with malt liquor. When I got my first pair of pointe shoes, I broke them in by practicing a barre routine at the East River, holding onto the fence that prevented us from falling into the murky water when we drank beside it, scraping the pink satin along the filthy concrete.

And, true to my plans to educate myself better than Bard could, I read, a lot. I gave myself assigned reading lists that I took very seriously, starting with classics like *The Master and Margarita* and *East of Eden*. I read history books, focusing specifically on New York City counterculture, and got really into French existentialists. Camus' ideas about absurdity fit perfectly into my justifications for not taking life seriously—why would I go to school if nothing really matters?

Eventually I branched out into whatever interesting paperbacks I found for cheap from the street vendors on Avenue A.

I picked up a used copy of Volume I of Anaïs Nin's diaries from my favorite vendor for $4, and fell in love. In a journal from that time, I wrote, "Anaïs Nin's writing has shown me the possibilities of writing about one's own life as artistic expression." After reading her diaries, I started carrying a notebook with me constantly. My favorite places to write were on a covered stoop while it was raining, or an empty subway car in the middle of the night when I wasn't actually on my way anywhere. I wrote some terrible, dark poetry about wanting to die and feeling dead, but mostly I wrote about the desire to write—lots of iterations of "I feel like there's something important I have to express but I'm not even sure what it is, let alone how to put it into words."

And I wrote about my father. I wrote about how I was terrified that someday I would forget the little details: the sound of his voice, the way the skin around his eyes crinkled when he smiled, his smell, the goofy face he made when he knew he was being funny. I wrote about how much I missed him and how I still couldn't comprehend the fact that I would never, ever see him again—not even when I needed him most. Not even when I was grown up and had children of my own, his grandchildren, who would never get to hear him read a Grimms' fairy tale or learn from him how to use watercolors with a light, decisive hand so they don't get muddy. Once it was all on the page, I still missed him just as much, but I felt a little less like I was choking.

I looked for any way I could find to stay connected to my father, and the most tangible way I could think of was to read his books. I had a stack of them on my shelf, and I read them like they could open a door to a conversation with him. I imagined him handing them to me, one at a time, with an enthusiastic recommendation and a wink, like when I was little.

He had a habit of using bus transfers as bookmarks, little clues that told me that, for example, on Tuesday, October 8, 1996, he was reading Chapter 11 of *The Marriage of Cadmus and Harmony*, Roberto Calasso's retelling of Greek mythology. Knowing exact dates made a kind of internal time travel feel more possible, as I pictured my father on a fall Tuesday, reading about Odysseus while riding an S.F. MUNI bus. A moment both humble and mythic, and so perfectly him.

He wrote cryptic notes in the margins, which I read even more closely than the books themselves. Next to a passage about how the mythic hero needs the monster "for his very existence, because his power will be protected by and indeed must be snatched from the monster," my father wrote "poet + poem."

I knew he had a great respect for poets, and sometimes discussed his sculptures as an attempt at poetry, but reading that note I wondered why he thought of poets there instead of sculptors like himself. I made a mental note to read more poetry, pulling the Rilke and Dickinson out of the pile of my father's books for later. I imagined him riding the bus, his shoulders hunched in his leather jacket, taking a mechanical pencil out of his breast pocket to make a note about how the artist doesn't exist without art any more than the hero exists without a monster to slay. I wanted to feel that way about something, and wondered if someday writing might be my monster.

When I finally worked up the courage—or desperation—to read my father's notebooks that night five years later and found them full of only his work, I felt cheated. I thought there must be something more, somewhere. Something he'd left behind that would let me have a conversation with him across time and death.

The notebooks still in a pile on the floor, I took out everything else I had of my father's and laid it all out next to them. I pulled his books down from my shelves, spread out the stack of his papers that had been sitting in a box all this time. I took out his jacket and put it on, the stiff leather hanging off my shoulders, much too big. It felt so much like a hug from him that I crumpled into it, crouched on the floor, trying to fit my whole body inside.

In the pile of papers, I found a clipped review from the *New York Times* of a 1984 group show at the Whitney called *Modern Masks*. Highlighted in yellow, I read: "Joseph Schactman builds on a sense of trust, using the imagery of dogs, but his papier-mâché dog heads, muzzled and covered with patches of fur, are like packs of wolves champing at the bit."

Nobody called him Joseph in real life, always Joe. The fact that he used his full name professionally, a nice Jewish boy getting his name in the paper, made me smile.

Two of these masks hung above the front door of my apartment, my guard dogs. There used to be so many of these masks. Some have disappeared to time, abandoned or sold, a few hanging in the homes of family friends. One of the two I have is cardboard, painted to look like a husky, perfectly round and slightly abstracted. The other has a papier-mâché snout, a particleboard wing coming out of the side of its face, and a long, tangled ponytail of human hair. The one with the ponytail also has the delicate mouth of a human woman, which is what I liked most about it when I first saw it as a child—I always wanted art to be "pretty," a preference I was forgiven because I was a little girl, while my father spat at critics, gallery owners, and collectors who shared it.

After reading the review, I went out into the hall. Still wearing my father's leather jacket over my pajamas, I stared at the masks, there over the door, trying to see them anew. Trying to really see them, not the way you see something that's in your peripheral vision every day. I stared at them like they might tell me something, like if I could stare deep enough into the holes of their eyes, I might find my father's shining blue ones peering back. But the masks just stared back with the stern, calm facial expressions of bodyguards.

I never knew my father had work at the Whitney, but it felt like proof that at some point, someone out there had known how important his art was. I never for a moment doubted his legitimacy as an artist—when I picture my father, his hands are always busy carving something with his pocket knife, or drawing in a sketchbook. When we read Greek myths together, Hephaestus was the god I pictured with my father's face. The descriptions of him, forging his masterpieces at the foot of Mount Olympus, always dirty, but the most tender and pure-hearted of them all—those were clearly stories of my father. I can't always remember the sound of his laugh, but I can remember the exact curve of his shoulders as he hunched over his work table, concentrating so hard on whatever he was working on that I'd have to say "Papa!" three or four times before he heard me. He was fully committed, living his art like a bird lives the sky. But I know he never got the commercial success he wanted and deserved. I remember a few gallery shows, but mostly he made work not to sell but because he couldn't help himself. He was never deterred by the lack of swarming fans, but I'm sure his artist's ego wanted more.

In one of the notebooks he wrote, "As I'm working, + as I'm used to the fact that it's working for the drawer, I do pretend that someone (a pretty girl) will see it."

I imagined him going out to buy the paper the day that *Times* review came out, playing it cool, not wanting to let people know how excited he was, but quietly clipping it out and saving it between vet bills and torn-out museum-catalogue pages. And I was amazed that the reviewer understood something so essential about these masks—that the serene, steadfast quality of a loyal pet and the ravenous, threatening growl of a junkyard dog are not contradictory in my father's work; they're both essential, and in harmony.

I realized then with a jolt that *of course* it wasn't in the notebooks that my father had left traces of himself behind for me—it was in his work! His work, which he'd spent a lifetime pouring himself into, and which was right there in front of me, on my walls and shelves all this time. It was so obvious I started laughing, loud, until I was half laughing and half crying, doubled over in the hall. This was why I'd wanted to be alone for this endeavor.

Some people grow up with religious iconography, I grew up with my father's art. Instead of saints or crosses or scrolls, I had dogs, deer, rabbits, and the female form. Deer with human hands for antlers, dogs leaping into space, rabbits in targets, rabbits in burrows, rabbits in the sky. They were my sacred images, created by the dirty, calloused hands of my alchemist father.

I learned the language and stories of my father's art before I learned nursery rhymes. I knew that the women he drew were my mother, and that he drew her because he loved her and couldn't believe how beautiful she was. I knew the deer and dogs and rabbits were him, that the hands he sculpted were modeled after his own hands. I learned to draw by copying his drawings, learned to work clay by playing with his discarded scraps. I learned to understand the world around me by trying to recognize what my father might think was beautiful—understanding that every walk we took was a scavenger hunt, and that anything could be sculpture material.

Everyone inherits their parents' stories, their baggage, the symbols through which they interpret life. But perhaps this is especially true and inescapable for the children of artists, who are steeped in it and surrounded by it in such a literal sense—growing up in homes decorated with tangible pieces of our parents' psyches externalized.

In his copy of *The Language of Fire*, a collection of literary criticism by Maurice Blandchot, next to a line that claims that the written sentence can "reduce the heaviness of things to the agility of signs," my father wrote in pencil "and sculpture? who's [sic] business is the 'heaviness of things' or 'the heaviness of things as signs + agile?'" He was arguing in the marginalia that sculpture can turn life to symbols too, but it uses heaviness to do it rather than resisting the heaviness of human existence—capturing our experiences and thoughts and emotions, bringing them down to the solid earth like a wild bird in a cage. All the intangible parts of him that I was so afraid to lose were right there, captured in the heaviness of his work.

My father had left me the letter I wanted so badly after all, it was just in code—all I had to do was decipher it. I knew what some of his images represented, but I didn't know how they all fit together, how one led into the next, or exactly when he started each series. If I could figure out what was going on in his life when he made each piece, I thought, maybe I could read his sculptures like a story. Maybe I could almost hear my father's voice.

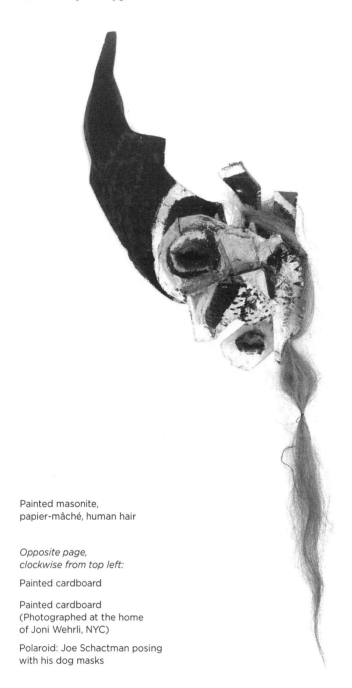

Painted masonite,
papier-mâché, human hair

*Opposite page,
clockwise from top left:*

Painted cardboard

Painted cardboard
(Photographed at the home
of Joni Wehrli, NYC)

Polaroid: Joe Schactman posing
with his dog masks

In the same box of papers as the *Times* review, there was a postcard for a solo show of my father's work at a gallery called Civilian Warfare. This seemed like as good a place as any to start. I searched online and, as I expected, the gallery had closed years ago—disappeared along with most of the East Village's once-vibrant art scene. But I found the gallery's former owner, Alan Barrows, and sent him an email, asking if he remembered my father.

"Joe's work was really disturbing. I loved it," Alan told me when we met for drinks a few weeks later. I'd suggested the bar tucked away upstairs from the Public Theatre on Lafayette. It was dark in there, with big banquettes you could recede into. It felt like a place where it would be safe to expose my biggest vulnerability and ask a stranger to tell me who my father was. I liked Alan right away because not everyone uses the word "disturbing" to describe art they love, but people often use it to describe my father's.

Alan remembered the dog masks, and one sculpture in particular called "Dog Carcass." Alan laughed in bemused appreciation, describing the plastic tubing my father had spray-painted red to look like guts spilling out of the wire figure, with scraps of fur glued onto it. Industrial carnage. The sculpture is listed for $2,000 on an old price list, but it didn't sell. I don't know what happened to it.

"We had a reputation for showing the most difficult work in

the East Village," Alan remembered, explaining that during the neo-expressionist craze in the early-to-mid '80s, scary, ugly art was in. This was my father's heyday. I closed my eyes for a moment while Alan spoke, and tried to time travel.

Coming out of the economic disaster that was 1970s New York, rent was cheap in the East Village. It was dangerous enough to be relatively undesirable, but not dangerous enough to scare away artists looking for space to live and work. There were galleries everywhere—124 galleries opened in the East Village and the Lower East Side between 1981 and '86, I learned later—and in the early days, most of the people who went to openings were artists who had shows in the other galleries, the art scene a self-sustaining ecosystem.

"Artists just wanted to applaud each other's efforts," Alan said. "It was a great time because it really wasn't about commerce yet. It was really like we made a show for ourselves and other people happened to come."

I did some research into the East Village art scene in the decade before I was born and discovered that ABC No Rio, a place that felt so very mine, had opened in 1980 and was a leader in the alternative art space scene of the time. My father probably spent time there. I wondered if he sat in the same corner of the backyard as I did; if he took classes there or showed work there or just hung out and found his people there, like I had when we first moved back. I wondered if that's why I was so drawn to that place, a trace of him there, a frequency that my animal-self recognized as home, like salmon swimming toward the place of their birth.

This idyllic world of artists supporting each other's work, able to live and create in the city before gentrification swept them all away, is a land of myth. This vibrancy and grit is what people have been flocking to New York City for ever since, chasing the faintest whiffs. But I could see in Alan's eyes as he described that era, leaning in over the candle at the center of our table, where we sat just a few blocks from where his gallery used to be, in a bar with $14 cocktails, that he was describing an Atlantis—a world so long gone it's sometimes hard to imagine it was real at all.

There was also a dark side to that utopia of grime: with as many shooting galleries as art galleries in the East Village, heroin was everywhere. "It was part of the fabric of the neighborhood," Alan said. "It always seemed like it was outside our group. Until the people who were using stopped being able to control their habits and it became very obvious."

Alan told me about his business partner, Dean Savard, one of the people who had kept his habit hidden until he was too far gone to keep up the pretense.

"Heroin was one of the things that made our gallery go out of business," Alan said. He explained that Dean became unreliable, often absent—either on a bender or in rehab—and that once word got out, investors and collectors didn't want to put their money in the hands of someone who might spend it all on drugs.

Alan didn't know until years later that my father was involved with heroin, and neither of us knew, when we spoke, if he'd been using when they knew each other. I only knew about the time when my father's addiction was out in the open, making his teeth fall out, getting him arrested. But of course it was there, lurking, before that, just like it had been with Dean. Heroin is insidious—it doesn't destroy all at once. It rots a person, slowly, from the inside out, so that by the time you can see the damage, it's often too late.

I was relieved that Alan didn't know my father as a junkie. That part of him didn't have to enter the story yet. I knew that if I kept digging, I would eventually have to look directly at my father's addiction. If I really wanted to know him better, I couldn't gloss over the ugliest parts—but that didn't mean I had to run straight into the darkest bramble. My father's addiction was never the first thing I thought of when I thought of him, never the first thing I told people about him, and I didn't want it to be the first thing I filled in the details of, either.

After drinks, Alan and I went to the opening of a retrospective of Greer Lankton, an artist who showed at Civilian Warfare around the same time my father did. On the walk to the gallery, Alan described her work as "big, freaky marionettes." I didn't know what to expect, but my interest was piqued.

I'd never been to Participant before, but if felt so familiar as soon as we stepped into the gallery. The lighting, the sounds. The smell of paint and wine. I wondered how much more of my adult life would be spent in galleries if my father were around to cajole me into going with him. I realized it had been over a year since the last time I went to an opening, and felt a pang of guilt for not maintaining a presence in my father's world. When I was a kid, I didn't know any adults who weren't artists, didn't know there was such a thing. There was always an opening or a gig to go to, and when we visited my parents' friends, I was never plopped in front of a TV or handed plastic toys; I was set up with watercolors or clay or collage materials, or hiked up onto my father's hip to look at the new work the adults were appraising together. This was the world I was born into, but I had abandoned it. When people ask me if I'm an artist like my father, I get defensive about writing being an art. But the truth is that he'd be sad if he knew that I hadn't drawn or painted anything in years. I made a mental note to dig the charcoals out of the bottom of my desk drawer when I got home.

As I stepped into Participant, I was flooded with a memory, hazy but visceral: I was about five years old, small enough that the adults milling around towered over me. I was at a gallery opening, much like this one, standing in front of a piece of art I had decided I liked. I don't remember what it was, but I know that as a kid I liked anything that reminded me of either a princess (anything with a female form) or my cats (anything animal). I was standing in front of it, very serious, hands clasped behind my back in my best impression of Adult Person Contemplating a Piece of Art. The space behind me is watercolor in my memory, blurred and vague, but the sounds are the same gallery sounds I was hearing now: hushed voices accumulating into cacophony, heels clicking on a concrete floor. The smell was the same blend of paint and wine.

I was wearing the red Mary Janes I'd painted with silver glittery nail polish and dubbed ruby slippers. I refused to take them off, even to go to bed. My mother would wait for me to fall asleep and carefully remove them, leaving them where I could find them quickly in the morning.

I remember looking up and saying something to the adults about what I thought of the art. I probably used words too big for my face, but I was dead serious. I don't remember exactly what they said in response, but I remember that they found my critique adorable, coming as it did from within a cloud of blonde Shirley Temple curls. They laughed, they might even have insulted me with an "aw," and spoken to each other about how sweet I was as if I wasn't standing right there. But I didn't want to be adorable, I wanted to discuss the art. I scowled at them, an expression I've been told my whole life is an exact replica of my father's scowl—all eyebrows—which I'm sure only endeared them further. Just as I felt my cheeks start to heat up to match the red of my ruby slippers, my father walked up behind me. I heard the thuds of his work boots and saw them come into view, covered in paint—he never dressed up for galleries, though sometimes if it was his own show he'd buy a clean t-shirt from the drug store on the way there.

"What do you think of this one, Lilly?" he asked.

When I told him I liked it, he asked "What do you like about it?" as he always did, probing for what had led me to my conclusions and teaching me to articulate critical thought before I started kindergarten. He was genuinely interested in what I thought, what it was about a piece of art that appealed to my young mind, unadulterated by critics and academics.

I blinked and remembered that I wasn't five years old, standing with my father; I was an adult, blocking the doorway of Participant. Alan was gesturing to a huge marionette with bloodshot eyes, a square jaw, swinging breasts, and a flaccid penis. "See?" he said. "Yeah," I nodded.

I took a few steps inside to get out of the way. Looking around, I noticed how many of Lankton's pieces looked like dolls and puppets and felt certain that my child-critic self would have approved. And they were strange and vulgar—anatomically correct sets of intersex genitals, close-ups of penises leaking period blood, bald, "masculine" faces with heavy make-up and exposed ribs—so my father would have liked them as well.

I wondered if Lankton and my father knew each other, and figured that they probably knew *of* each other, at least. The bonds formed in those days were strong—even thirty years later, Alan seemed to know everyone in the gallery as we squeezed our way through the packed, narrow space. He introduced me to each person we greeted as "Joe Schactman's daughter," getting an unsure look of vague memory from a few people and emphatic exclamations of "Oh my god, seriously?!" from others. One woman, who looked to be in her fifties, with the classic older-artist-lady look of unruly hair and one too many scarves, seemed to choke on the words, saying she remembered when I was born, that she loved my father so much.

"Wow," she said, starting to recover herself and blinking at my face, clearly seeing him in it, as people so often do. "So, how is Joe Schactman doing?"

I paused and blinked back at her a few times. I'd gotten used to saying "He's dead" automatically and without much emotion when people asked me about my father in passing conversation, as if I were saying "he's a sculptor" or "he's a Taurus." But this was the first time in the years since his death that I'd actually had to say those words to someone who knew him, informing them for the first time that their old friend was gone.

After a few seconds too long, I answered, "He died. In 2000." I winced after I said it, not wanting to see the surprise and sadness on her face. She told me she was so sorry, and I excused myself as quickly as I could. The whole thing already felt dreamlike: this crowded, brightly-lit space full of few familiar faces from around the neighborhood, plus a handful of people who knew me because they knew my father but who I'd never seen before, all milling around and between Lankton's bizarre sculptures. Having to break the news of my father's death as if it had just happened made the surreality of it all start to feel less curious and more distressing. Suddenly the crowd wasn't bustling—it was claustrophobic.

A second person asked me how my father was "doing these days," and I thought I might have a panic attack, my mouth wrenching into a nervous chimp-like grin and my throat constricting. I didn't know whether or not I'd stayed the polite amount of time, but I found Alan and gave him a quick thank-you-I'll-be-in-touch hug, and shoved my way outside like I was at a punk show rather than a gallery opening. I breathed in as much of the cold autumn air as I could as I darted between cabs, across Houston Street and toward home.

Dropping out of high school felt like a triumph at first, but it was lonelier than I expected. Most of my friends were still in school, which meant they couldn't wander the streets with me until sunrise every night. So I did it alone.

Sometimes when I found myself on an empty subway platform late at night with a train barreling through the tunnel, I had to concentrate to keep from stepping in front of it. There was no logical thought, no actual intention; just a sudden, intense desire to casually step in front of a train and die. It scared me. I'd thought that moving back to New York would make me feel better, I'd thought that dropping out of school would make me feel better, I'd thought that drinking my blood-volume in malt liquor and cheap vodka would make me feel better, but nothing did.

I considered reaching out to my mother, once, even though we were barely speaking and I mostly avoided her. I thought about writing to her, like we did in Fort Ord, about how even when I was laughing with my friends, there was a deeper part of me that was just screaming. I thought about telling her how I never slept, how I didn't want to kill myself but I was afraid I might anyway.

Then she slit her wrists in the middle of the bodega on our corner with the shards from a beer bottle she'd dropped. At the time, and since, all she's offered by way of explanation is that she just saw the shards on the floor and did it without thinking. I didn't make the connection at the time that this was an impulse I could relate to; when she told me, I thought it sounded ridiculous.

My mother had been trying to outrun her demons since she was a scared little kid in foster care. Heroin had kept them at bay for a while, but she got clean when I was seven and had never found a replacement buffer. She'd moved in with Tom the same year she left my father, and now she was on her own for essentially the first time in her adulthood, struggling to pay rent in one of the most expensive cities in the world, trying to make a living by selling her clothing designs, with a teenager who screamed at her all the time. She didn't know how to cope. I don't blame her now for being overwhelmed, but I did then.

I was used to being in our apartment alone while she stayed over at her new boyfriend Robert's place two blocks away, and even for a ten-day stretch once when they took a trip to Morocco together, but being there alone while my only living parent was on a 72-hour psych hold at Bellevue felt different. I noticed the quiet in a way that I never had before: the water rushing through ancient pipes behind thin drywall, the muffled conversations of neighbors. I sat on the futon couch that also served as her bed when she was home, unsure what I was supposed to do. I tried putting music on but it felt too loud compared to the quiet. I climbed into my loft bed, above the kitchen, and stared at the ceiling a foot away from my face, like a coffin.

I knew then that my mother was no more suited to save me than I was to save her. We were, each of us, alone. A small, hardening part of me knew she was supposed to be able to help me, but 'supposed to' didn't really mean anything.

I remembered the shared journal and how my mother had never been a solid thing I could hold onto. As I lay there in my bed, I looked deep into myself for any little part of me that needed her, and tried to hold my breath until it shriveled and died.

I wondered what would happen to me if she died, and realized there was a good chance I'd be sent to live with her sister Rachel, in Philadelphia. At the idea of being taken away from New York again and sent to live with my aunt who enforced a strict curfew for my cousin and supervised her homework, social time, and nutrition, I panicked. That was what scared me the most about the possibility of my mother killing herself just three years after my father died: that the courts might send me somewhere with rules to follow.

When she was out of the hospital, back home and not talking about what had happened, I told my mother she had to write a will saying that if anything happened to her, Hannah, my godmother who lived a few doors down from us on Ludlow Street, would get guardianship of me. "I'm not moving to Philly," I said, my voice deep and hoarse with the urgency I was trying to get across, everything I wasn't saying but hoped she would understand anyway; how if she'd cut just a little deeper with that glass she would have left me completely alone, and she owed it to me to at least sign a piece of paper so I could decide what that aloneness would look like. She let out a small and distant laugh, like she was abstractly aware of the absurdity of her fifteen-year-old daughter making her own emergency guardianship plans. "Ok, I will," she said. But from the tired, flat tone of her voice, I knew she wouldn't.

I mentally prepared myself in that moment to wriggle out of the state's custody if I ever had to, made a quick list of which essentials I would shove into a backpack, and started working up the courage to knock on the door of C-Squat and ask the squatters to let me move into any spare corner of their dilapidated building. I ran through possible scenarios: if I could move quickly enough, I could get out of there with my things and maybe even a few pieces of my father's art before the bureaucrats even realized they were supposed to do something with me. Or, worst case, I'd be shipped off to Philly where I could sneak out of my aunt's house in the middle of the night and beg for change downtown until I raised bus fare. However it played out, I prepared to be on my own, understanding that really, I already was.

After the surreal experience at the gallery opening with Alan, I told myself there was no rush, that I could spend the rest of my life learning about my father and I didn't have to go any faster than I could handle. That moment in the gallery, where everything blurred around me except for the woman who didn't know my father was gone, had brought my grief even closer the surface, like it was tingling just under the skin of my whole body. I was afraid to bring it out any further, so I tried to keep myself busy with college classes and bar shifts and friends.

But every time I stepped out of my bedroom, the dog masks above the door stared at me. Where before they had watched over me, now they were watching me—waiting, wondering when I was going to come back and finish the conversation we'd started. As months passed, I began to feel the same guilt as when my father had sent me a letter and I knew he was waiting for my response. I couldn't leave my questioning unfinished.

And while I was shaken by the gallery experience, I also noticed that in the weeks after talking to Alan and starting to put the dog masks into the context of my father's life, I could see his face in my mind more clearly. I could almost feel him near. It was a feeling I couldn't resist, even if it meant walking a narrow path high above a dark pit of grief.

So I called up Mark Rounds. Mark was my father's best friend from art school and his roommate for most of their young adult lives. They had the impenetrable, intoxicating bond of friends who were used to being seen as a pair: Mark and Joe, Joe and Mark. They spoke in coded jokes from their time living together, running a construction company together, converting an abandoned factory into a giant loft and workspace together. They had seemingly endless rituals around the shows they'd watch (*Hawaii 5-O*) and the scotch they'd drink (Johnnie

Walker), and were always talking about the next camping trip, the next road trip, the next big art project.

The review that mentioned the dog masks was from 1984, when I knew my father and Mark were living together in Brooklyn. So when I couldn't stand the expectant stares of the masks any longer, I took the Bolt bus from New York to Philadelphia to talk to Mark. When I got to his door, he was standing on the front steps, waiting to give me a big hug, enveloping me almost as completely as when I was a little kid.

When I was about two, Mark started dating my mom's sister Rachel, and became a stepfather to her daughter, my cousin Sabina. With her birth father out of the picture, Mark stayed in Sabina's life as her father figure, even though his relationship with Rachel was short-lived. So he's family to me on both sides; my double uncle, my non-religious godfather.

My earliest memory of Mark is from a roof-top barbecue in Brooklyn where he grilled chicken over coal, wrapped me in his giant flannel shirt when the sun went down, and sang along at the top of his lungs to the tinny boombox. I was enamored. When I was little and we would go see his band Mild Thing perform, he always made sure to dedicate a song to me, the only three-year-old in the bar. Later, when my mom and I would visit Rachel and Sabina in Philly, Mark would always come by and take us girls swimming, or to a movie, right when we were starting to go stir crazy with boredom after being in an apartment with our mothers for days on end. And when I first started to take my writing seriously, he took me out for a beer and told me, solemnly, "Be careful getting a job to support your art, because it's easy for the job to take over and not leave you any time for the art you wanted to support in the first place." It was a piece of advice that came close to satisfying my constant ache for advice from my father. I tucked it away in my mind, and I return to it still.

"Hey! How *are* ya?" Mark greeted me at his door, in the distinctive booming voice that made me believe him when I was three and he told me that Johnny Cash's voice coming from the boombox was his own.

Mark took my backpack and led me into the big open kitchen where a fluffy white cat was eating wet food out of a little ceramic bowl on the counter. He asked how my bus ride had been and grabbed two bottles of beer out of the fridge. As we settled at the long kitchen table, Mark opened one and handed it to me, before opening another for himself.

"So," I said, trying to sound casual even though starting this conversation felt momentous. "Tell me about when you first met Papa. I know you've told me some of these stories before, but...tell me again."

He chuckled. The way it came out of one side of his mouth, the way he looked down like he was keeping half of the joke to himself: a flash of my father. Mark reminded me of him so much—by association, by shared mannerisms. I felt the weight of the fact that this might be the closest I'd get to a real face-to-face conversation with my father. Big, Johnny-Cash-voiced Mark looked at his hands fidgeting in his lap and exhaled sharply before he started to speak, and I knew he was thinking a version of the same thing—carefully choosing his words, aware of the pressure of speaking for his friend.

"It all started at Tyler School of Art, right here in Philadelphia, back in 1976," he began, in an exaggerated *once upon a time* voice. He told me about how he and my father, who he sometimes referred to as "Joe" and sometimes as "your Papa," bonded over the pool table in the student lounge freshman year of art school, where they'd play during lunch and late at night; a love of biscuits and gravy; and Frank Sinatra's cover of "Winchester Cathedral." He said they used to sing it in a British accent, "for some odd reason I don't quite recall."

He told me about the classes they liked and didn't, the people they liked and didn't, and about the first apartment they shared, sophomore year. He told me about the stuffy still-life paintings Joe was doing when they met, and how he slowly developed his own style when he branched out and explored other mediums. And about how Joe went to a summer program at Yale before his junior year. "That was where he met Cathy," he said, off-hand, like of course I knew that already.

"Wait, you knew Cathy?" I interrupted.

I remembered whispers of the name Cathy from when I was a kid. Nobody had ever told me anything about her directly, but I'd heard her name spoken like a secret by the adults when they shared stories of the old days. Electric and hushed. Eventually I'd pieced together enough to understand that Cathy was a woman my father had loved before my mother.

As a child, the idea of a parent's first love, an alternate-storyline love, feels unreal, mythical. Now that I was searching for new ways to understand my father, the idea of his first love was more enthralling than ever. I was fascinated by the idea of Cathy; I wanted to sit down with her and have her tell me long stories about my father in those early days. I wanted every detail of what he looked like and sounded like back then, just entering adulthood, like I was now. I wanted a level of detail about his facial expressions and interests and particularities that only a lover would remember.

But I couldn't ask Cathy for these stories, because one of the very few things I knew about her was that she died a long time ago. But now, I thought, maybe Mark could bring her to life for me. And then I had another ghost to chase.

"Cathy Wehrli!" Mark responded enthusiastically. "We were all madly in love with her. She was just so friggin' cool. She was a stunningly attractive girl," he leaned in to confide, raising an eyebrow and nodding to make sure I got it. "Really, really, monstrously pretty."

He described her as "beautiful, blonde, rich, and reckless." Disappearing into a hall closet, he returned with a few photographs, one of Cathy and Joe, in the middle of screen-printing t-shirts. He looked so young in the photo, maybe 22—like we could have been in classes together. Cathy's back was to the camera and her face turned to the side so I could see less than her full profile, but it was enough to see her soft full lips and upturned nose, her square, Germanic jawline and short, shaggy, blonde hair. A wholesome, classical beauty, with that round quality of both Renaissance art and Middle America.

Mark told me about Cathy's husky, Travis, and how the first dog masks were based on him. I remembered the round-faced husky mask above my door, the one I'd stared at, searching for my father's eyes, and imagined it anew as a real dog he'd known. Imagining Travis, a loving pet with his tongue sticking out of his mouth, added a layer of sweetness to the mask, softening the mystery and unattainability of it. Mark said Travis was also the subject of many paintings Cathy and Joe collaborated on. The large-scale dog paintings they worked on together feel jubilant, full of bright reds and yellows, with dogs leaping across the canvases as if chasing tennis balls or soaring through the sky. I remembered staring up at one of these dog paintings as a child, not knowing the story behind it, following the shapes across the canvas as if they were animated.

Joe and Cathy made big, clunky bracelets and necklaces together out of trash, which they wore until they completely fell apart, not taking them off even to sleep or bathe. This trash-art jewelry must have been the precursor to, or maybe the origin of, the bottle-cap-and-razor-blade horseshoe crab pins my father was still making years later, which became a trademark. When I was little, if I saw someone wearing one of these pins, I knew that he had officially accepted them as one of "our people"—a highly selective and special group.

The one my father wore on his leather jacket would scratch my arm when he picked me up, so I called them "ow pins," which he adopted as their official name. He collected rusty bottle caps in a jar in his studio, and whenever I saw one on the street I'd pick it up, spinning toward him with triumphant glee. Every time, he'd say, "Oh, thank you!" with genuine delight. My mother didn't like me picking up trash off the street, but the excitement on my father's face outweighed the concern on hers.

"Ow Pin:" Rusted beer bottle cap, razor blade, with a safety pin set in putty on the back so it can be worn on a lapel

Joe and Cathy snuck into construction sites at night and left big sculptures for the workers to find in the morning—guerilla installation art. I pictured them on a chilly night, the traffic lights reflecting on dark streets, quiet except the occasional newspaper truck or scurrying rat. He'd be wearing a leather jacket, of course; maybe she would too, looking like Debbie Harry with her short bright hair. They'd have tools with them, and materials, probably in a canvas Army surplus backpack, which he called a knapsack. They must have scoped out the site during the day, knowing exactly where they were going. When they arrived at the chain link fence, he'd chuck the knapsack over first, looking around to see if anyone noticed the loud thud as it hit the dug-up dirt on the other side. A gentleman, he'd kneel down to give her a boost, weaving his fingers together into a step for her and helping her hike her weight over until she landed with an even louder thud. She'd laugh, the thrill of trespassing too much to stifle. Then he'd heave himself up, the fence jerking with his weight, making way more noise than it had when she went over with a boost, as the black steel-toed boots he wore every day, scuffed and creased, angled for a grip. When I pictured him landing I winced a little, remembering that he always had bad ankles. But if it hurt he wouldn't have let on. He'd pick up the knapsack and maybe grab Cathy around the waist and kiss her before they set to work. I wondered how much sculpture material they brought with them, and how much they relied on what they found on the site. They wouldn't have been able to resist stacks of fresh-cut boards and metal rods, cinder blocks and wire. Did they work fast like thieves, or linger and take their time, confident in their right to be where they shouldn't? Did they scurry away as soon as they were satisfied with their creations, or did they hang out in their new kingdom and appraise their work? Maybe there were cans of beer in that bag of tools, and they'd cheers triumphantly, sitting on cinder-block seats.

My father was always on the lookout for sculpture materials, his notebooks full of notes about exciting finds, which he called "obtanium" ("major obtanium: two large cow bones" or "great find today: sheets of newsprint paper"), followed by several pages of lists of possible ways to use the new material and notes on behavior he noticed as he started working with it. This way of looking at the world, like a giant art supply store ripe with possibility, was so central to who he was, and it started with Cathy. This was why Cathy was so important: She was his love and also part of his art, helping to invent his whole style and ethos.

But that didn't mean their relationship was perfect. Cathy had something to prove, a rich-girl-playing-the-starving-artist chip on her shoulder, Mark explained as he opened another beer. She was insecure, wondered if her trust fund made her a less authentic artist. Always sanctimonious, Joe did nothing to reassure her. I remember him being loudly dismissive of anything he deemed fake or unoriginal—he didn't even want me to have coloring books, expecting me to draw my own pictures if I wanted something to color in. This sounds so rigid and exacting now, but I don't remember pushing back against it as a child. *Okay*, I'd say, and draw elaborate outlines of princesses and their various exotic pets (parrots, lions, dragons) and then color them in with colored pencils, perfectly happy with my homemade coloring books. And then he'd ask me where the princesses were standing, why there was no background behind them, leading into a lesson about perspective and using the whole page. I can see how it would have been stressful to be his partner, to try to keep up, to always wonder if he thought you were doing enough.

After that summer at Yale, Mark said, Joe dropped out of Tyler and moved to New Haven to be with Cathy. I'd mostly been nodding along up until this point, taking notes, sipping beer, occasionally asking, "And then what?" But when I heard that my father dropped out of school because of Cathy, I sat up straighter, demanding, "Wait, what?" This was not the story I grew up with. All of that self-righteousness about how everyone in art school was taught to draw the same and think the same, and how he had to leave to preserve his own artistic integrity, his grand proclamations of the drop-out's honor, which I'd adopted and adapted for myself. And now Mark was telling me that the whole philosophy of "art school kills the artist" was actually just a cover for my father giving up school for a girl! My jaw dropped and I could almost hear myself saying "Papa!" in the exasperated voice I used as a kid when he insisted on eating half of my box of cookies "to make sure they weren't poison:" part outraged, part amused.

Thinking of the father I knew, who drew while I played in the playground, who talked a bigger game than anyone about commitment to one's work, I was stunned to hear that he dropped out of school for Cathy. And he was self-critical enough to be very aware of the choice he was making, to doubt himself before he chose love over his education. I started to think that even if the imagery had started with something as simple as Cathy's pet husky, maybe the dog he was depicting over and over wasn't really Travis—it was him. Following Cathy like a loyal hunting dog following Artemis into the woods. Maybe a little self-mockery, or maybe romanticizing and rationalizing the idea of following and devotion. And I was even more curious about Cathy than before. Who was this woman my father would put before his work?

I felt like I'd caught him in a lie, found the first little rip in the mythology of him. The real reason he dropped out of school may not have been a deep, dark secret, but it was exactly the kind of perspective-shifting, humanizing revelation that I'd thought I couldn't have without him here to talk to. And I was finding a way.

When Mark had told me everything he could remember about the love story of Joe and Cathy, he said I should call up Ken Selden for the rest. I remembered Ken from when I was little, one of my father's friends who I considered just as much my friend. But unlike Mark, I hadn't seen Ken since before I started elementary school. I knew I'd have to win him over, convince him I wasn't a little kid anymore—that he could tell me the whole story.

We met at Bar Six, a French/Moroccan restaurant near the New School; the kind of nice place students only went when parents were in town. I was in my junior year by this point, studying journalism and editing the student newspaper. I was steeped in the ins and outs of interviewing, bias, storytelling, and I felt ready to take on the story that had always loomed largest over my life. Part of me was afraid of what I might find, but I told myself it didn't have to be so scary if I thought of my father's life as just that: a story to report. A profile without access to the subject, like Gay Talese's famous piece on Frank Sinatra, written stubbornly and brilliantly despite the fact that the singer declined to be interviewed. I was beginning to imagine that these stories I was collecting would end up in a book—my father and his art immortalized. The idea that I could share my father's work with the world helped me stay motivated to keep digging—and I felt much less vulnerable as a writer doing research than as a grieving girl, searching for scraps of her father.

Ken and I sat at a little bistro table outside, watching people hustle up and down Sixth Avenue, just at the start of the evening rush hour. I ordered a French 75, a cocktail I had just discovered, and which felt convincingly adult. I wore a cardigan and my new glasses with clear pink plastic frames that, I thought, looked like glasses a happy, well-adjusted person would wear.

I recognized Ken immediately, but was surprised to see that he had aged. It's always a little jarring to see my father's friends looking older than he ever got to be. I expect the cool dudes in leather jackets, eyes glinting with the inside secrets of what's really going on wherever they are, confident smirks on their faces. I stared at Ken and thought how strange it was to see him middle aged, trying to imagine what my father would have looked like if he'd lived to his fifties.

After we hugged and made some small talk about his work and the last fifteen years of my life, I told Ken as succinctly as I could what I was trying to do: I was asking my father's friends all the questions I couldn't ask him, trying to put together a story of his life and his art, hoping to understand him better. I didn't mention that I was motivated as much by guilt as by curiosity, that I couldn't move forward in my life unless I found a new form for my grief by learning enough about my father to miss him in a new way.

I took a sip of my cocktail, flipped open my notebook, and asked Ken what his first impression of my father had been.

"It's amazing that we managed to become friends after the way we met," Ken said. Apparently, Cathy had a habit of breaking up with one boyfriend by showing up somewhere with a new one—and the way she broke up with Ken was to bring Joe along when she went to visit him in D.C.

"She just showed up with this other guy and still wanted to stay with me," Ken shook his head at Cathy's brazenness. "Eventually I realized Joe had no idea, so I didn't hold it against him."

I didn't know that Ken and Cathy had dated, but was excited about this new avenue to get to know her—asking my father's old girlfriend's old boyfriend for insight into her as a way to learn something about him was roundabout, yes, but I would take what I could get.

There was a film series on the Yale campus when he was a student there, Ken told me, and he got the idea to make a little money by setting up a stand and selling bags of popcorn before the movies started. One night, this beautiful blonde girl came up and said she wanted to work in the popcorn stand with him. I pictured her, hair shaggy and short like in the photo Mark had showed me, accentuating her broad cheekbones. Leaning on the counter, her face close to Ken's.

He let her into the tight space, and right away she noticed the bag of cocaine that Ken had tucked under the corner of the popcorn maker. "It was like she had a radar," he said. Cathy mentioned the coke, and Ken said, *Take as much as you want.*

"She proceeded to dump out the entire bag and do the whole thing in one line!" he said, leaning back in his seat, still a little stunned more than thirty years later, shaking his head and laughing at the absurdity. "She looked up with a smile after doing every last speck of the coke and said, 'What? You said to do as much as I wanted!'"

Seeing Ken still charmed by the story of their first meeting, how awed he was by her boldness, her hot-girl-getting-away-with-it act, made me think I knew her type. I wondered if she had known all along that it would be there—if she'd heard from someone who heard from someone that Ken the popcorn guy had coke, and if you flirted a little he'd probably give you some. I knew that kind of girl. I'd *been* that kind of girl.

The year after I dropped out of Bard, when my life revolved fully around the park and my friends, Jael ran away from home. At first, she stayed with me in my loft bed above the kitchen on Ludlow. I knew where to press on my mother's soft spot for girls who didn't feel safe at home, and she agreed, even though space was already tight in our studio apartment. But we lived just ten blocks from Jael's dad, and when "Have you seen this girl?" flyers went up around the neighborhood with her picture on them, she decided to go farther, to Boston. Rakhel decided to join her—maybe for the adventure; maybe out of a sense of protectiveness, not wanting Jael to go alone.

I'd always been the one to move away, leaving friends behind and starting over somewhere new. Knowing we'd probably move again soon, I'd never gotten too close to anyone in San Francisco or Carmel or Buffalo or Marina. But now that we were finally back home in New York and I planned to stay put forever, I had formed true, deep bonds with these girls. I was unprepared for how much it would hurt when someone else did the leaving.

Haley felt abandoned too—Jael had been her best friend since middle school. Our mutual hurt bonded us closer than ever until we became an inseparable pair, dressing the same, talking the same, spending every day together. Before, the five of us had been a sub-unit of a big, sprawling network of teenage punks and "park kids," but when Jael and Rakhel left, Haley and I clung together and interacted with everyone else less.

We'd all tried coke together, but Haley and I both liked it more than the rest of the girls. When our little group fractured and we started spending most our time together, alone, there was nothing holding us back.

Most afternoons, I woke up to Haley's face inches from mine, saying, "Get up get up get up," her hand shaking my shoulder. A heavy sleeper, I never heard her coming in, using the keys I'd given her. My mother didn't seem to mind Haley letting herself in every afternoon, probably because she wanted me to wake up and get out of the apartment as badly as Haley did.

Haley leaned against the counter, rapping her long nails on it impatiently as I stumbled around, eyes half-closed, groping through the pile of clothes on the little bench under my loft, looking for something to wear. I pulled on our daily uniform, almost identical to what Haley was already wearing: ripped tights, teeny-tiny homemade miniskirt, black tank top, steel-toed Doc Martens. "Come on, hurry uuuup," she said, starting to stomp her feet a little as I painted thick layers of black liquid eyeliner around my eyes and ran wet fingers through my almost-waist-length curls, dyed auburn now. Finally, I sloppily applied some red lipstick, and we were ready to go.

We ran down the three flights of tenement stairs before bursting onto Ludlow Street, each with a Lucky Strike filter ready between our lips. We leaned in and each lit the other's cigarette with the matching black mini-Bics we kept in our bras, a little ritual of mutual chivalry. Then I made the call she'd been waiting for me to make this whole time, the reason for her impatience.

He went by Prince. I knew his number by heart—I still do, all these years later, from dialing it so many times on my Nokia brick phone. I never saved the number—a half-baked precaution. I asked Prince to meet us at the usual spot and he responded, "Half an hour," before hanging up. We marched arm-in-arm to the corner of Ninth and First, talking too loud, walking too fast, smoking too much. That teenage girl attitude that we thought said *we don't give a fuck* but really said *please look at me*.

We waited on the corner, chain smoking, until Prince pulled up and I got in the front seat. While he drove around the block, I snatched up the three grams of coke he'd left in the center console, replacing them with six $20 bills, and he dropped me off back where we started. I always said a friendly goodbye and thank you as I got out of the car, like he was a cab driver. He smiled and waved and said, "See y'all tomorrow."

I don't remember if we ever discussed who would do it, but I always made the call—always got in the car, always carried the drugs. It was understood, if never explicitly said, that I had less to lose than Haley did.

She'd lived in the same apartment on 11th Street for her whole life, and she went back there at the same time every day to two parents who were not only both still alive, but also still together, waiting for her with dinner on the table. She wanted to be wild and dangerous, but only until curfew. I wanted to get out of my body, to find the limits and see if reaching them would finally make me feel calm. Getting arrested or robbed wouldn't have changed my life that much, so I was the one to step into the line of fire. Plus, since I was still fifteen and Haley was sixteen, I had a better chance of avoiding a criminal record if I ever did get arrested.

We asked the bartender at St. Dymphna's on St. Mark's sweetly if we could use the bathroom, and when he gestured toward the back, we scurried in together. I locked the door behind us and checked it twice, while Haley closed the toilet and sat on the lid, taking the notebook out of her purse and laying it across her lap. I took the first of the three bags from Prince out of my bra and set it on our makeshift table. She held the notebook steady on her lap with two hands, her long, spindly, silver-heavy fingers tightly grasping the edges while she tried not to let her knees shake. I pulled out the pocketknife I'd bought at the Army surplus store on Houston Street and named Mitch.

I dumped half the bag onto the notebook and used Mitch to methodically break it up into a fine powder, with no chunks to hurt our sinuses. I divided it into four perfectly, neurotically even piles, and shaped each one into a neat, even line. One for each nostril. I tried to be fast so the bartender didn't have time to wonder what we were doing in there, but not so fast that any powder fell to the floor.

When I was finished, we each pulled a pre-cut plastic straw from our bras. I lifted the notebook carefully, steadily, from Haley's lap and held it up for her to go first, and then we alternated. Deep inhales and exhilarated, overwhelmed exclamations as we threw our heads back to feel the chemical explosion at the backs of our throats. Giggly jitters when we were done, as we rushed out of the bar wiping our noses and avoiding the bartender's eyes. We liked to say we were in love; we just did coke instead of having sex (although we also made out sometimes, mostly in mosh pits).

The bemused smile fell from Ken's face as he explained that Cathy's drug use didn't stay light-hearted and charming for long. After she graduated from Yale in 1978, Joe and Cathy moved from New Haven to Manhattan, to an apartment on West 27th Street, back when that neighborhood was more *Taxi Driver* and less High Line. When I imagined their apartment, I remembered the photo Mark showed me of them printing t-shirts and expanded the space around them in my mind—the big table that was probably scavenged plywood resting on pilfered sawhorses, string crisscrossing the room with clothespins for hanging anything that needed to dry: shirts or photographs or paintings. The Talking Heads playing, loud, out of a boombox splattered with paint. Probably no furniture other than a futon on the floor, and maybe some mismatched chairs they found on the street. Art supplies everywhere. Plastic buckets of interesting scrap metal, canvases leaning on every wall. Maybe one corner for wood to carve and a dedicated wall for in-progress paintings. I pictured them moving through that space together, dancing and goofing around, maybe working on one piece together or maybe spending hours a few feet away from each other not talking, each fully absorbed in their own work, coming together at the end of the day to show each other what they'd accomplished. To critique, and, most importantly to an artist, to witness the new work and celebrate its existence. Love and art and life all in harmony.

But she was using more and more, and moved on from coke to heroin. Soon her habit became her defining characteristic, eclipsing those Debbie Harry cheekbones and that bewitching cool-girl sway. Heroin took over all of the space in her life that used to be for love and art.

Hearing this, my heart started beating faster as I wondered if she and my father discovered heroin together. If this was when he started using. There was a flare of anger at this woman I never met as I wondered if maybe she introduced him to it. And then guilt at my anger, as if someone could ever be responsible for another person's addiction, as if a strung-out 22-year-old offering her boyfriend a hit could possibly comprehend that she was starting a chain of events that would someday shatter his future daughter's life.

There was a hesitation in the way Ken paused after certain sentences, looking at me to gauge my reaction, clearly wondering how much I knew. I tried to assure him that he could speak freely by asking point-blank, as casually as I could muster, "Do you know if he was using then, too?"

Blood pulsed in my ears but I kept my face calm. I was trying to approach the darkest corner of my childhood with the cool distance of a reporter. On the surface, I was kind of pulling it off, I thought, but my mouth was dry, my pulse loud and everywhere.

A part of me felt like if I knew exactly when he first started using, if I could conjure a mental image of where he was and who he was with, I could reach back through time and beg him not to do it. If I could pinpoint a beginning, maybe the end would make more sense. But I also knew what a long shot it was that I'd ever be able to ever nail down a precise date—it was such a long time ago, many of the people who were around then are dead, and the ones who are still alive were high at the time. Plus, there's no telling whether he was upfront with friends about when he started using and how much. I remembered what Alan said about people keeping it under wraps, how he didn't even know about his business partner's habit until it was full-blown.

David Carr wrote in *The Night of the Gun*, his investigation into his own years as a drug addict:

> To be an addict is to be something of a cognitive acrobat. You spread versions of yourself around, giving

each person the truth he or she needs—you need, actually—to keep them at one remove. How, then, to reassemble that montage of deceit into a truthful past?

Carr at least had his own memories to measure others' accounts against, as admittedly inaccurate as those memories were, visible only through a dense fog of inebriation and self-delusion. I had only the montage of deceit to work with.

"It's possible," Ken said, but he wasn't aware of Joe using heroin until a few years later, in the mid-'80s, when, he said, "It was something we all did occasionally." I made a note that this meant my father was using when he was showing work at Alan's gallery after all, he'd just still been able to hide it.

Me bringing up my father's drug use first seemed to put Ken at ease, and he lost the tentativeness in his voice as he told the rest of the story of Cathy's deterioration.

"It was really, really ugly at the end," he said. "In a way, what she was doing was closer to suicide than a drug habit. Her arms were getting infected." She blew through all of her family money. She tried to get roles in porn films to feed her habit, but she had track marks covered in puss-filled abscesses, and not even the sleaziest underground pornos would cast her. No more cool-girl sway. Just wasting away. Rotting while still alive.

"Joe tried to help her," Ken said with the sad faraway voice of knowing how useless it was. Maybe he was thinking about the irony of my father trying to help someone get clean, when so many people tried and failed to help him later. I was.

I remembered the *Times* review of the dog masks that I knew my father made either during or soon after this time with Cathy, "like packs of wolves champing at the bit," and wondered if that's how he felt trying to wrestle her away from addiction. Hunters bring dogs with them into the woods not just to track prey, but to ward off predators.

A dog will fight a bear if it's threatening its master. Dogs don't care that bears can rip them open with one claw, that they don't stand a chance. They'll arch their backs and growl, snarl, and even charge to defend the person they love.

I imagined that same scene of the two of them in their apartment on 27th Street, canvases still leaning on every wall but now the same ones that had been there for months, untouched. I didn't hear the Talking Heads anymore, just him pleading with her to stay there with him instead of going out to score. Trying to pull her toward him like he used to so naturally, but her pulling away, getting frantic with her craving and impatient with him for trying to stall her. Him showing her a new drawing he'd done, huge, on a fresh canvas, saying he needed her help with the colors, and wouldn't she like to try out those new paints, and work on this piece with him? Her, exasperated now, scoffing and saying something cruel before stomping out, slamming the door. Him throwing the canvas across the room, trying to be louder than her, but too late.

Joe even brought Cathy with him to St. Louis once, to his parents' house, to dry out. He didn't explain anything about it to Barry and Phyllis, his buttoned-up, suburban Jewish professor-and-housewife parents. Just, *We need to stay for a few days*, and his first love convulsing and puking and shitting her withdrawals in his childhood home.

They got back to New York and she got high again right away, Ken said. And she got angry at him for trying to stop her. He said it with a shrug, but I understood. Junkies don't see it as help, they see it as control. My father would learn that later. As I imagined him pleading with her, making ultimatums, yelling and crying, I wished he could have remembered later what it felt like to be on that side of it, watching someone you love fall apart. I wished the memory of that heartbreaking helplessness could have been enough to make him stop. But then I was just doing the same thing to him that he had done to

Cathy, trying to apply logic to addiction, where it has no foothold. I should have known better.

In between ducking into bar bathrooms to do lines, Haley and I walked. Even faster than before, in lockstep, linking arms. We walked up and down the avenues, zigzagging down streets at random. At this point we avoided the park, where all of our other friends were, because we were having "HaleyLilly time," living in a sacred bubble for just us. We didn't want to let anyone else into our time, and none of them wanted to talk to us, either. They said we were annoying when we were like this, and sometimes that they were worried about us. We blamed our friends for judging us, never stopping to wonder if maybe they had a point; if maybe two underweight, underdressed teenage girls prattling on about the best bathrooms in the neighborhood to get high in, telling the same stories over and over, and synchronizing our cigarette inhales and exhales, might be unbearable to be around, and might be cause for concern.

Our friends didn't want to hear our stories anymore, but that was fine; we told them to each other. We told each other stories about our childhoods and our dreams and our nightmares, and we told each other stories about things we'd just recently done together. "Remember that time that creep followed us around all night, so we beat the crap out of him in the pit at CBGB?" "Remember that time Mike Schein called us backstage to help him with his costume, and everyone else in the audience was so jealous?" Remember that time, remember that time, remember that time…telling and retelling until every moment we'd shared became legend.

This was our routine almost every day. As often as we could afford between my waitressing tips and the money Haley had saved from her summer job. Then she'd go home for curfew, and I'd spend the rest of the night coming down, anxious, twitching, chain smoking, walking in circles around the city.

On the days we didn't do coke, we talked about doing coke. We paced and tried to find ways to distract ourselves, but mostly we just talked about how badly we wanted to get high, planned out the next time we could, and fantasized about becoming famous models so we could afford as much coke as we wanted.

When Jael and Rakhel went to Boston, Jael had left her guitar with Haley and Rakhel had left her bass with me, for safe keeping. Haley and I were so angry at them for abandoning us that when we sold their instruments to buy coke, we told ourselves it was justified and that we were doing it out of anger, not desperation.

This didn't look or feel like addiction to me. Addiction, as far as I knew, meant getting arrested and going to rehab, meant broken marriages and rotting teeth and nowhere to live. This was just a couple of kids having fun. My standards for what qualified as a problem were severely skewed. So what if I craved coke every day and only really felt like I was having fun when I was on it? So what if I woke up every morning with my sinuses burning and the taste of death in my mouth, and the only thing that could make me feel better was more? This was still nothing like what my parents had been through—it wasn't even in the same league. So it didn't count.

I also convinced myself that cocaine was harmless compared to heroin. For the most part I'd try anything I could get my hands on—I took random prescription pills just to see what would happen, dropped acid whenever the opportunity arose, smoked crack in the bathroom of the Knitting Factory…but heroin was the one leap I couldn't bring myself to take. It was the bright line that separated fun from danger; as long as I didn't cross it, I would be fine.

On yet another day that started with Haley shaking me awake and a call to Prince, we crammed into a bathroom stall together at Sidewalk Cafe, years before I worked there, and did a couple of extra-huge lines.

She sat on the closed toilet, a notebook on her lap. I stood facing her, back against the stall door, and cut the lines. We were fast, efficient, practiced. We walked out wiping our noses and laughing too loud and thinking we were being slick when we were actually being as obvious as it's possible to be.

By the time we got outside, my throat was starting to close up. We lit our cigarettes, and Haley immediately doubled over and puked into the gutter, just bile and a few sips of water. We both sat down on the curb, where she kept puking, and I rubbed her back while I focused on trying to breathe, even though it felt like my chest was full of cement. My vision was a pinhole. I don't know, still, if we just did too much or if it was a bad batch, but in that moment, I had a realization that felt like it might be the last thought I ever had: *I'm an addict.*

After a few minutes, or maybe an hour, of sitting there in the literal gutter, clasping our sweaty hands together and silently focusing on staying alive, we both managed to come back to something resembling breathing. Hunched over, our ribcages showing through our skimpy shirts like stray dogs and our faces bloodless under our smeared makeup, we didn't need to see the looks we were getting from passers-by to know we looked half-dead. We laughed and cried a little with relief and shock, lit two more cigarettes, and got up to start walking again.

That day, we acknowledged out loud for the first time that we'd been doing coke almost every day, that we were miserable when we didn't have it, that all we talked about until we got it was how and when to get it again. We admitted to each other that we were addicted.

Now that I knew that I wasn't just doing coke for fun but that I'd fallen into that same trap I spent my childhood watching my parents try to climb out of, I couldn't do it anymore. The part of me that wanted to not repeat that pattern was stronger than the part of me that liked being high.

The test of my own willpower, to stop that very day, for good, was also, subconsciously at least, a way of proving to myself that it's possible to be stronger than addiction. That my parents could have done it too, if they wanted to. I told myself that while my little teenage coke habit never got anywhere as severe as their addictions did, it could have gotten that bad if I'd let it—but I didn't. I quit cold turkey, just like that. And I felt smug about it, even as I sweated and shivered in bed for three days, telling my mother I had the flu. Maybe a more generous view is that I was subconsciously trying to heal old patterns—letting this same story play out in a different way so I could imagine a different life for my parents and myself. That might have been true, but closer to the surface was a petulance, a *was that so fucking hard* defiance. Saving my own life out of spite.

After a year of trying and failing to fight off Cathy's addiction for her, Joe had to face the fact that his choices were to either leave, or stay and watch her slowly kill herself. So he left.

I pictured that same 27th Street apartment again, most of the canvasses gone now, sold for drugs and no new ones painted. His single suitcase packed, next to the door. Maybe he made a big show out of packing up his things, hoping she would stop him; that she would promise to get clean, that's she'd say the right things so he could let himself stay. Or maybe she did beg and promise, but he knew better than to believe her. Or maybe she just watched, high and detached, not saying anything at all when he paused at the door, looking back at her one more time.

I wanted to go back in time to stop him as he walked out that door and say, *Remember how you feel in this moment. Don't let this happen to the people who love you.* I wanted the memory of Cathy to have been enough to keep my father from losing himself to addiction, like the memory of him had stopped me. But it's so much messier than that. His example made me turn back before it was too late, but it also helped me rationalize myself onto that precipice in the first place.

Maybe when my father started using he didn't realize he was in danger because his habit wasn't as extreme or dire as Cathy's had been. I wanted witnessing her deterioration to have scared him straight, but why would I expect that when I knew firsthand that it could just as easily have helped him justify his own habit as relatively "under control?" It's so easy to believe that you must be fine when you have the worst-case scenario to compare yourself to.

Ink drawing on paper

Joe left Cathy in their apartment on 27th Street and moved back to New Haven, where he started going to a bar called Ron's Place. The Ramones played at Ron's before they were famous—and later so did Blondie, the B-52s, and the Talking Heads. By 1980, when Joe arrived, the little hole in the wall with a pink awning was a well-known hub—New Haven's CBGB. He partied with all the young punks, his black jeans rolled up over his work boots, white t-shirt tucked in, a little swooped pouf of thick brown hair and a mole on his cheek that I would later call his "beauty mark," which always made him laugh. He moved in with the members of a local punk band, Disturbance, who played at Ron's regularly: Tom Hosier, Bud Lyon, and Jason Cook.

Lake Place, as they referred to their apartment, was a huge party pad, Bud told me when we met for crepes and sangria at The Crooked Tree on St. Mark's. They covered the walls with band and movie posters, along with spray-painted stencils and found art. The Lake Place crew were literal starving artists, subsisting off of shared leftovers from various shitty restaurant jobs. They lived together five, six, ten to an apartment because that's what they could afford while spending the majority of their time making music and art, and that's the way they wanted it.

Joe was living what he thought of as the authentic life of an artist, the ideal he'd criticized Cathy for not living up to. If he could only afford either paint or food, he would always choose paint. He was proud to go hungry, because it was proof of his dedication, even if he was only proving it to himself.

Joe hitchhiked a lot during those New Haven years. Bud remembered him regularly taking off with a backpack and a sly smile, coming back weeks or months later with wild stories and full sketchbooks. He was testing himself; testing his self-sufficiency, his grit. Like an ancient rite of passage where a boy goes out into the wild alone and, if he survives, comes back a man. I can see him standing on a highway somewhere, squinting into the distance like a young Clint Eastwood. Reveling in the uncertainty and the possibility.

I wanted to hitchhike so badly when I was a teenager. I felt all the same impulses I think he felt then: a desire for nature, fate, chance, challenge, triumph. An escape from the mundane and into the truth of being a human animal, trying to stay alive and creating a path as you're on it, through improvisation and ingenuity. I couldn't bring myself to ignore how dangerous it would be for me to hitchhike alone, and going with a companion would have broken the spell, so I never went. But I like to imagine my father's travels, thinking that they're in my DNA and that maybe what I felt back then wasn't desire, but memory.

When he'd been in New Haven a few months, Joe started dating someone else. Bettina, who everyone called "Tink," was seven years younger than him. At first this didn't sound like a big deal to me; my mother was nine years younger than him, age is just a number, et cetera. But then I did the math and realized that when they met, he was 23 and she was sixteen. I remembered being sixteen, remembered the decent older guys who treated me like a little sister and the sleazy ones who took my word for how mature I was, who went along with the make-believe that a sixteen-year-old girl is a grown woman just because she says she is. She'll always say she is. But she's not.

I wondered if my father would have thought of Tink if he'd lived to see me at sixteen, the guilt catching up to him once he saw the truth of that age. But as I condemned him, I also rationalized, thinking of how young he was at 23, collecting garbage and turning it into jewelry to give to his friends. I thought of him reeling from having to walk away from Cathy. And of how some arbitrary age cutoff would've had no place in his life of trash-art punk-rock freedom—just like it had no place in mine when I was sixteen, going to shows in the last of the dingy punk venues in the East Village and never once getting carded for drinks.

In a picture of Tink from the year they met, she's wearing an oversized Army jacket over a paisley dress, crouched down in the grass, petting a dog. Her hair is super short—not in the cool, new wave way that Cathy's hair was short, but short like a barber cuts a boy's hair. She's squinting with the studied seriousness of youth; she looks like someone I would've hung out with in Tompkins.

I moved out of my mother's apartment at sixteen. Not into a squat like I'd planned, but into a flimsy new-construction apartment in Bed-Stuy, directly across the street from the Marcy Projects, with three friends. I was too young to legally be on the lease, and the Hasidic landlord wouldn't shake my hand because I was a girl, but I didn't care. It was mine.

I waited tables at a dingy little Italian place on Ninth Street called Café Gigi, where the owner blasted Tom Jones so loud it scared away the customers who might've settled in for date nights, and where I once drank a cappuccino I'd made for myself during a lull only to discover a dead cockroach at the bottom of the cup. I canvassed for the Working Families Party in the middle of winter, trudging through February snow, getting doors slammed in my face, and getting paid in commission. I commuted on the bus every weekend over the summer to the renaissance fair upstate in Tuxedo, selling leather goods for $9 an hour. I worked as a dominatrix in a "dungeon" tucked away in a midtown office building (wearing leather goods from the ren faire that I got as commission bonuses). I got my first bar job at seventeen, cocktail waitressing Friday and Saturday nights at a rowdy Irish bar on the Lower East Side, carrying trays of Jäger shots high above my head and pushing through dense crowds of frat bros and neighborhood ruffians. I worked my ass off to pay rent when I could have stayed with my mother for free, but it was so worth it. I listened to Billie Holiday sing *God bless the child who's got his own* every day, and felt like I had arrived.

I found a coffee table on the street in the East Village and carried it on my back on the L train, and then the G, to put in the center of our shiny new living room. We got two couches for free from somewhere and set them up facing each other on either side of the coffee table. My roommates, Mike, Sebastian, Phee, and I all came home from work every day and sat on those couches, drinking cheap beer by the six pack, smoking gigantic blunts, and taking turns choosing the music to blast. Friends came over almost every night, celebrating the novelty of an apartment that wasn't just free for the weekend while parents were out of town, but really truly ours all the time—referred to universally as simply "the Apartment."

The Apartment quickly started to show signs of housing a bunch of teenagers who had never lived on their own before: stalemates about who should do the dishes until the kitchen was so disgusting we all just avoided it, crusted splatters on the bathroom floor, overflowing ashtrays, and empty bottles covering every surface like a thick, glass moss. But I kept my bedroom at the end of the hall clean and perfect; scrubbed the floor, dusted the windowsill, and hung my father's art on every wall, surrounding me as I slept. I reveled in the freedom to get fucked up and make a mess as much as the others, but for me this was also an opportunity to create a home that felt like real solid ground. This was a chance to stop feeling like I had to be ready at any moment to make a break for it if my mother killed herself or got committed or kicked me out when I finally got on her very last nerve. This was stability, safety; this was everything. It was the best possible version of the on-my-own-ness that I'd been preparing for—not surviving on the street hiding from social workers, but building a real life for myself, on my own terms.

So even when we partied for days straight and smoked blunts with breakfast and played a game we called "ketamine wheel-chair Olympics" in the Apartment's long hallway, I still kept my room clean.

Almost a year into living in the Apartment, I got a call from Jael. She'd hooked up with an older guy named Jim in Boston and they'd gotten "married" by branding each other's wrists with heated liquor bottle caps. They'd hit the road together, visiting us in New York briefly and then heading to the Appalachian Trail, where they lived for a while—and where Jael got pregnant. They settled in Florida to have the baby, and less than a month after their daughter Riley was born, hurricane winds tore the roof off the trailer they were living in like it was a tin can. Rather than getting his new family to safety, Jim blamed Jael for everything that had gone wrong for them, raging and thrashing while she curled her body protectively over their three-week-old baby. Jael had had enough, and called me. She didn't tell me the whole story, just that she and Riley needed somewhere to go. I told her without hesitation, without consulting my roommates or thinking about what it would be like to have an infant living in my room, to come live with me.

When they arrived, I hung the art postcards my father had sent me above Riley's crib, so she would always be staring up at beauty. I convinced my boss at Café Gigi to hire Jael, and we switched off—one of us waiting tables, the other home with the baby.

I changed Riley's diapers and walked around the house holding her gently to my chest, bouncing her and whispering to her for hours so that she could sleep. I continued to pace long after she'd drifted off, smelling the sweet smell of her baby hair and not minding the drool that inevitably covered my shoulder. I read to her at night, just like my father had read to me.

I felt so much older than I was, world-weary even, coming home from a long waitressing shift, cracking open a beer and massaging my sore feet, only to hear the baby crying and heave myself back up to tend to her. So my idea of being sixteen is a little skewed—but still, I felt a protectiveness toward Tink when I thought about the age difference between her and my father.

I talked to Tink on the phone late one night instead of doing my homework, a few weeks after I talked to Bud. I sat at my desk, like I was a reporter conducting an official interview. But as I asked her what my father was like as a young artist, what she thought of him when they met, what it was like to date him then, I felt more like a teenage girl, talking on the phone to another teenage girl, about a boy.

"He never got over Cathy," she said, "idolizing her completely the entire time we were together—I was too young to realize the extent to which this was bad for me. Given his obsession with Cathy I've never understood what I was to him—a pet? I was surly and unhappy. How was that fun for him? A protégé?"

She said the art he was making then was all about Cathy, trying to make something bold enough, wild enough, that it would draw her attention away from heroin and back to him, back to art, back to the world they had created together. I wondered if he knew this was what he was trying to do, or if his sixteen-year-old girlfriend understood his heartbreak better than he did.

After I hung up with Tink, I climbed into my loft bed. My fat orange tabby cat curled up in my armpit, purring, and I fell asleep thinking about art as a way to try to be loved. My father was so principled, talked so much about the artist's responsibility to himself and to his craft—the hero's monster to slay—but, at least for a short while, he was also making art as a way to cry out to his lost love. Creating himself, hoping the woman he loved would be drawn back to him if he created a big enough, bright enough version.

I started to think of everything he made as a call, waiting for a response. Not always from Cathy, not always necessarily from a specific person at all—but from somewhere. And right as I drifted off, half asleep, I had a moment of crystal clarity that with all of this searching, I was trying to respond.

In the summer of 1981, about a year after he left Cathy, Joe hitchhiked through Mexico. He'd been gone about a month when he called Lake Place one night just to say hi. Bud told me they'd been waiting for his call so they could tell him that Cathy had overdosed and died.

I thought immediately of the moment I found out my father was dead, how all light and sound collapsed in around me. I wondered how he handled that blow when it came for him. I imagined him, a young man out adventuring, skin tanned and clothes dirty. Stubble on his face, smoking hand-rolled cigarettes. Light and free and living his life. And then *boom*.

Did he fall to his knees on the street in whatever Mexican town he was in? Did he yell "no" over and over again, like I did? Did he think maybe he had misheard, that maybe he could go back and hear it differently? Nobody was there with him, and Bud couldn't remember who'd actually broken the news, so I'll never know how he responded.

But I do know that he got drunk, passed out on the beach, and got robbed of everything he had with him—it was a story I'd heard him tell, but without the context of why he'd gotten so drunk on that particular night. I pictured him sitting in the sand on an empty beach in jeans and a flannel shirt, staring out at the moonlight reflecting on dark waves, wondering what he could have done differently to save her, taking big swigs straight from a bottle of tequila. And waking up in the morning, baking in the sun, his mouth as dried out as the sand, his pockets looted, the memory of the news he'd gotten the day before as harsh as the morning sun.

Hearing his adventure stories as a child, I pictured him as the hero in one of the Westerns he loved so much—his John Wayne impression was spot on—but placing this one in the context of his grief over the death of his first love, he no longer sounded like a cowboy but like a sad, lost boy.

After Cathy's death, his work changed. He abandoned the color palette she had introduced, the electric blues and yellows they used when they painted together, the spray-paints and bold splashes. Mark remembers that everything turned to gray tones and browns—the palette he would primarily work in for the rest of his life. The dark, natural tones of dried leaves and unfinished wood, of concrete and scrap metal and lead.

And this was when he first started making art out of dead things. He'd been working with found objects for a few years, but now he introduced roadkill. He would sneak into the Yale libraries and Xerox dead birds, and then draw over the Xeroxes, creating multi-layered images of women with real bird wings. A black-and-white photo from the time shows him standing on the side of the road, wearing a plaid shirt and a cowboy hat, triumphantly holding a mangled dead bird from one wing tip. His face is boyish, a *look what I found!* expression.

Joe with roadkill

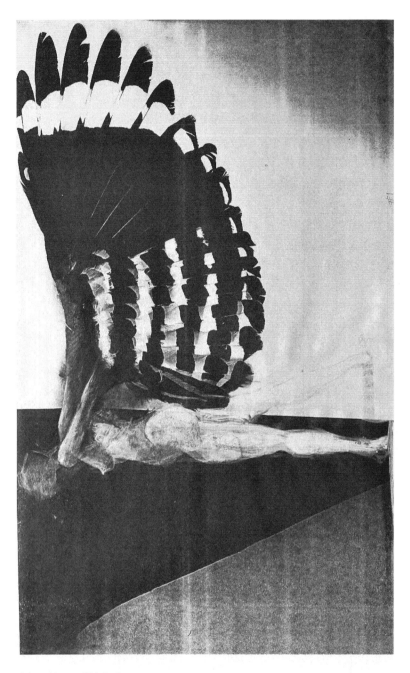

Ink on Xeroxed bird wing

I once carried a festering bird carcass on a Greyhound bus to make my father happy. When I was nine or ten, my cat killed a hummingbird. I wrapped it in several paper towels, put it in a Ziploc bag, and carried it in my travel bag on the three-hour bus ride I took from the Central Coast up to San Francisco to see my father on weekends. My mom had packed a peanut butter and banana sandwich for me to eat on the bus, but when I saw the two Ziploc bags next to each other, I lost my appetite.

It was worth it though. When we got to his apartment, I immediately took out the bag with the hummingbird in it, careful not to hold it too tightly because I didn't want to feel its little feet through the paper towels and plastic, and handed it to him. He looked surprised, and a little skeptical, when I told him to open it. As he carefully lifted the paper towels off of the tiny corpse, he let out a breathy, "Wow!"

He was thrilled with the gift. He made a wire cage for the dead bird, which he hung outside his bedroom window so it could decompose without stinking up the apartment. He would eventually turn its bones and wings into sculpture material.

Even after his death, dead things always appear to me as presents for him. While I grew up with his ow pins, I didn't see a real horseshoe crab until I was thirteen and my father had been dead for just over a year. I was walking along the beach when I spotted it, right there in my tracks: a giant, rotting ow pin tangled in seaweed. Marveling at how accurately nature had imitated my father's work, I picked it up with an inside-out plastic bag, careful not to touch the sharp spines that used to scratch my skin.

I thought of how happy he'd been when I brought him the hummingbird, his beaming face clear in my mind as I stuffed the mangled, too-fleshy ow pin into my bag alongside my water bottle and sunscreen. The stench of rotting sea-life was overpowering, especially for a squeamish, vegetarian adolescent girl, but I had to collect this real-life Schactman piece and bring it home, ignoring the cognitive dissonance of a gift for a dead man.

My father did the same thing after Cathy died, his art a series of gifts for a dead woman. He continued the guerilla installations they had started together, making sculptures and then abandoning them, letting them deteriorate. He took a trip out to the woods upstate and left sculptures hanging in trees, photographing them before leaving them to the elements. The process of rotting in the woods was the last stage of the development of these pieces, like paint drying or glue setting; their destruction was their creation.

I always thought that these pieces and his interest in how they changed were all about his enjoyment of materials, his curiosity about how they behaved over time. But learning that this work started when he was mourning Cathy, it felt clear that they were also about loss. He was creating sculptures that would "die," making his grief tangible.

Before I had ever experienced loss, my father taught me to surrender the things I'd made. When he took the bus down from San Francisco to visit me in Carmel—the trip he wrote about in his notebook—we walked to the beach that was just a few blocks from where I was living with my mother. Carmel Beach is breathtakingly gorgeous, the kind of beach that's photographed to advertise California tourism. I loved that beach, but I spent a lot of time there being lonely, resenting my mom and our move to the quiet seaside town, missing my father and feeling like I didn't belong. But with him there, I felt like it was finally okay to really enjoy this magical place that was practically in my backyard.

We walked around collecting shells for a while, and then started playing a game, at his instigation, where we drew pictures in the sand with long sticks as quickly as we could and then watched them be erased by the lapping waves. I drew mostly abstract shapes, maybe a couple of cat faces, but his trained hand managed to create animals in motion, fleeing the tide. We had only a few seconds for each round of drawing before a new wave would rush over it, soaking our legs and erasing our work like a giant Etch A Sketch. It was a game that involved a lot of shrieking and running, but underneath the playful surface was a valuable lesson in impermanence.

The work he made after Cathy died was about deterioration and letting go, but it was also about holding on. He conjured her over and over again in his artwork by making the things they had once made together. He continued to draw and sculpt dogs, though they were tortured, like he was. He showed them surrounded in darkness or starved near to death, with their ribs showing—or eviscerated, like the Dog Carcass piece that showed at Civilian Warfare. He showed them hanging by the waist from ropes, suspended and helpless. He'd gone from the loyal companion following Cathy to New Haven, to the ferocious guard dog fighting to save her from addiction, and finally ended up grizzled, abandoned, near death. The last stage in the evolution of the imagery of his first love.

As I thought about how much art he made about and for Cathy after her death, I couldn't help but draw the parallel; I was doing a similar kind of conjuring here: art as a spell to raise the dead. Creating him on the page like he created Cathy in his studio. Writing my grief into these pages to make it tangible, so it would exist somewhere outside of me and I wouldn't have to drag its weight with me always.

As I pieced together the story of Joe and Cathy, how my father watched heroin destroy his first love, powerless to help her, and how deeply he grieved when she died, I couldn't shake the quiet but insistent voice in the back of my mind demanding to know how he could have let the same thing happen to him. I felt a painful tug as what I learned about Cathy started to shift what I knew about my father.

I remembered how I knew he was clean when he died because he'd told me so, and the vindicating autopsy report. No drugs in his system meant drugs hadn't killed him. I remembered how I'd repeated the phrase "undetermined causes" and been comforted by the lack of a clear answer, because that meant it wasn't the one answer I couldn't bear. And I wondered: Did it, really?

The first time I talked to my father about heroin, I was eight. When I stayed with him on weekends after my parents split up, he slept on the carpeted floor of the room he was renting, and I slept on the bed. He would watch with pursed lips while I carefully brushed the plaster and sawdust, metal and pencil shavings from the dingy sheet before lying down, occasionally commenting that I had inherited a fear of dirt from my mother, as if it was a weakness of character from which he was lucky not to suffer.

Across from the bed, under the room's one window, was my purple desk that we had found on the street. There were small chips in the paint, so we went to the drugstore and found a nail polish just the right color to patch it up.

I would sit at this desk and work diligently when we played a game he invented called "Studio," where we both "pretended" to be artists sharing a studio space, each working on our own projects. While we worked, we would listen to either Bach or Miles Davis or, on the few occasions that I wore him down, No Doubt. Studio was a way to keep me occupied so he could work, but it also created some of my best memories of him, an approximation of what it might have been like to spend time with him as an adult, in comfortable silence, both of us working.

He worked on his sculptures, and I attempted to make myself a pet robotic dog, with a wire skeleton and a paper-towel-roll digestive tract. The kid version of his Dog Carcass sculpture, though I had never seen it. I also made my first-ever carving, a princess, out of a bar of soap, which my father suggested as a good practice material. He showed me how to use a chisel— "Like this," he said, miming a smooth downward gesture away from his body, an angle that would make it nearly impossible for me to stab myself if I replicated it properly. He trusted me to be careful with potentially dangerous tools—though when he taught me how to use a table saw he joked that maybe we both needed adult supervision.

On the third wall, next to the door, was the stack of milk crates he used as a bookshelf. One day, I pulled out one of his big hardcover art books that I loved to pore over, looking for paintings of beautiful women to inspire my princess drawings. Probably Rembrandt, Renoir, or Sargent. As I flipped through the book, I found a piece of tinfoil tucked between the pages. It was folded into a square, with several small circles burned into it.

I often pretended to know less than I really did about grown-up things going on around me—partly so that adults would continue to be candid and I could learn more, and partly to avoid the awkwardness of them crouching down to have serious conversations with me—but I had a vague understanding that my parents were addicts. I idolized super-smart girls in books like *Matilda* and *Harriet the Spy*—I was the kind of eight-year-old who could figure out what a methadone clinic was for.

I knew that addiction was a problem my parents were dealing with, but I didn't differentiate it from the other grown-up problems they worried about, like paying rent or keeping the house clean. I knew enough to understand that drugs were bad for you, but in the same abstract way I knew that broccoli was good for you.

Playing innocent, I held up the piece of tinfoil and asked in my sweetest voice, "Papa, what's this?"

He didn't answer right away. He looked hurt, like when I told him I didn't want to try out a new drawing technique. It was a look I worked hard to avoid, and one that could get me to change my mind in an instant, to draw or paint or read whatever he wanted me to. The look I later imagined might have been the only thing that could have convinced me not to drop out of high school. After some deliberation he answered honestly, "That's from doing drugs," and then dishonestly, "but it's from a long time ago. It must have just gotten lost in that book." He wanted to tell me the truth, but also didn't know how to admit his weakest, lowest parts to the little curly-headed girl who stared up at him like he glowed.

Then I guess the guilt got to him, and after another long pause he told me that actually it was recent—but that he had stopped again, and he was doing better. I believed him, and appreciated him not talking to me like I was a kid. He came over and kissed the top of my head, surrounding me in the smell of tobacco and plaster, and then we went back to playing Studio.

After that, there was a shift. Now he understood that I was watching, that I knew what was going on. Over the next couple of years, I would ask him about it even when there was no tinfoil to arouse my suspicion. He started telling me honestly how his efforts to get clean were going. He didn't use the word "heroin," or even the words "drugs" or "addiction," but I would ask how he was doing, and he would know what I meant.

"Really well," he would say. "I'm healthy." Or sometimes he would say he was "dealing with some stuff," or that he was "not doing so great but going to get better again soon." When he eventually went to inpatient rehab, he apologized to me over the phone and said the doctors were helping him there, making it so he could stay "healthy" when he left. And then there were those last phone calls, where he assured me he was healthy and we made plans to camp under the redwoods. We had our code, and it worked, and I'd never doubted—even when the adults did—that he'd been healthy when he died.

As a teenager, I was angry at everything but him. My father was the beloved lost, blameless as a saint, while I blasted my anger like buckshot at my mother, at teachers, at truant officers and cops and store owners.

Even when my teenage rage slowed to a simmer in early adulthood, I thought of my father's death as something that had happened to him. Cruel and random. But then I learned about Cathy, and started to doubt the murky, once-comforting half-truth about his death that I'd clung to for so long.

Slowly, over time, creeping up on me, sneaking in through trap doors, a realization started to form. As I walked to the store I started to question what I knew for sure about my father's death. In yoga class, I thought about how vindicated I'd been by the autopsy report, how angry at Audrey and everyone who'd assumed it was an overdose. Sitting on my couch drinking coffee, I thought about the last ten years of my life, when I somehow believed that my father's mysterious death had nothing to do with his drug use, and how I now knew that he'd started using by the mid-'80s at the latest, likely the late '70s, off and on until just a few months before he died in 2000. And I felt like a fucking idiot. A 43-year-old man's organs don't just shut down for no reason. And the damage done by poisoning yourself for two decades isn't instantly reversed the moment you stop. Then like an electric shock I wondered if it was even really true that he was clean when he died. I'd held that win so tightly and for so long that it had turned into a hard, resentful little stone in the core of me. Was it even real? My mother could have lied to me about the report; I'd never read it myself.

I didn't explain why, I just told my mother I needed to see the autopsy report. I knew she'd never throw it away, that it was stashed somewhere deep in a box within a box in the back of a closet. She knew I'd been looking for information about my father, and didn't question my request. It took a few days for her to find it, and when she did, she photographed each page and emailed the images to me, because she was upstate and I was in the city, and I couldn't wait until the next time I visited. I was wrapping my head around the realization that drugs had probably killed him slowly, eating away at him until his heart stopped pumping, but I still needed his death to not be something so careless and avoidable as an overdose. Something that hinged on one moment's miscalculation, pouring out just a little too much powder. That would be unbearable, so small an action tearing this gash through my whole life.

I didn't read the photographed pages too closely, trying not to let the image into my mind of his body, naked, being cut open. His chest cracked. His heart, exposed to the air, still and cold.

Sitting at my desk, my bedroom door closed and my cat on my lap for reassurance, I scanned past details that would call to mind cutting and dissecting, looking for the word "Toxicology." When I found it, I zoomed in on the photo of the page on my computer screen, but I also squinted my eyes so I couldn't quite read it, not ready for the plot twist I'd braced myself for. As I found the word "Heroin" in the left column, I reminded myself that my mother wouldn't have just sent this off to me with no explanation, no preparation or apology, if the word in the right column was "Positive." But then, she might have started to believe the lie after all these years if it was one. Looking at the screen sideways, out of the corner of one squinted eye, I took a deep breath and held it as I traced a fingernail across the screen, from the word "Heroin" to the word "NEGATIVE." There it was, typed in solid black letters. Irrefutable.

I felt relief, but also a twinge of doubt, a needling question of whether it really made a difference whether the drugs killed him all at once or little-by-little. The outcome was the same.

I scrolled down to the word "UNDETERMINED" across from "Cause of Death," and wished I could go back to when that had been enough. But undetermined cause doesn't mean no cause. And once I'd made space for the knowledge that it had to be the drugs, I couldn't go back. I started, for the first time, to see my father's death not as something that happened to him, but something that he let happen. A suicide of neglect, like a lie of omission.

It took a little while to sink in, but when it did I was flooded with anger. Anger like water so hot it feels cold. Anger that I had never before let myself feel toward my father. My understanding of him, of the world I lived in and the course of my life, had always been that he would be here with me if he had a choice. But now I felt like he hadn't tried hard enough to stay. Like he could have saved me from all of this grief if he'd really wanted to—if he'd gotten clean sooner, and stayed clean. And then I was crying hot rage tears, screaming into my pillow, realizing how furious I was at him for leaving me. Realizing that I'd been furious at him for half of my life, and I never even knew it.

I was shocked at myself for feeling such anger at an addict, as if addiction were a simple issue of willpower. It went against everything

I consciously believe about addiction. I believe in decriminalization and treatment, and needle exchanges, and decreasing stigma. As a teenager, at a time when I barely cared about anything, I volunteered for an organization committed to legalizing ibogaine, a controversial treatment for chemical dependency. I had wandered haplessly into the foothills of addiction myself, and not even noticed it happening. I knew my father's addiction was not a choice. But the anger was there, and no amount of logic could touch it. It came from the part of me that doesn't speak in words or understand rational thought. And after so long of not even knowing it was there, I couldn't ignore it once I discovered it, like not knowing you have cancer until your lungs are overgrown and twisted.

In discovering my father and Cathy's story, in learning about this grief that so deeply marked his life, I was finally able to see my own grief more fully, allowing it to be complicated by anger. Like it's easier to give advice to a friend than it is to know what to do in your own life, easier to recognize when a friend is being mistreated than it is to stand up for yourself, I could only see my own loss clearly by looking at my father's. I could see that Cathy had left him, that she wasn't just taken from him by some external force. I could see that he would have felt abandoned, betrayed, and angry underneath his grief. And I finally saw that I felt all of those things, too.

Cathy may have been woven into the dog imagery in my father's work, but as I saw my own grief reflected in their story, saw him lose her like I'd later lose him, I was thinking of his deer sculptures.

In a long-running series called Hunter/Hunted, my father drew and sculpted deer, often with antlers that were also human hands. Hunter/Hunted is about duality, the pursued and the pursuer both contained within one being. The enemy within as an inescapable fate like in a Greek tragedy; as inevitable as death, as natural as the hunt. The mythic hero who doesn't exist without his monster.

Cycles of self-contradiction, and self-destruction.

Floating near the bottom of a page of one of my father's notebooks is an idea for a sculpture: "The fall: Adam, Eve, the 2 trees, + the serpent, all intertwined as one entity." The biblical Hunter/Hunted.

I saw Hunter/Hunted in the story of Joe and Cathy; the repeating, self-containing, inescapable fate. He was the hunter, reaching out for his lost love; and then he was the hunted, just out of my grasp. I thought about the cycle of my father trying to save Cathy, seeing heroin destroy her, only to let it catch him later, and I was reminded that seeing and hating addiction didn't make him immune to its pursuit; that "he should have known better" is, of course, too simple. He did know better, but that didn't save him. Addiction is a hunter contained within the hunted, an enemy you can't run from because it lives inside of you.

I don't know if my father was intentionally depicting the relationship between his drug use and his attempts to save Cathy in the Hunter/Hunted series, or if it was more abstract for him. But whether that was part of the intention or not, this imagery helped me understand why seeing what happened to her didn't save him from the same fate. It helped me to not blame him quite so harshly.

I pulled all of the deer prints out of the huge flat file in my closet and pinned them up so they covered my walls like cave paintings. I could almost read them as a story: deer faces cut into maple leaves, deer profiles with human hands—my father's hands—coming out of their heads, deer and leaves and hands and deer and hands and leaves and deer. Fleeing, chasing, being caught, escaping, hiding…

I meditated on deer for months that would turn into years.

I saw Hunter/Hunted in the fact that I set out in pursuit of my father, tracking him through the story of his life and his art, but what I found was a new path into my own grief and anger. Like walking outward in a labyrinth and finding yourself again and again at the center. I wanted to tell his story, but at each new turn I found my own: ways that my story repeated and mirrored his, and important ways that it diverged. Following his story and finding mine inside of it, I was writing my own addition to the Hunter/Hunted series.

Carved wood; 10.5″
(Photographed at the home of Heidi O'Donnell, Phoenicia, NY)

I started looking more intentionally for the overlaps and resonances between his story and mine. Like one sweltering afternoon when Riley was about two, and a big group of us were sitting in Tompkins. I glanced over at Riley crawling around in the filthy grass, her golden hair plastered to her little pink face with sweat—the filth had never bothered me until I saw her crawling in it and then sucking on her fingers.

I scooped Riley up and strapped her into her stroller, throwing her things and mine into the basket under the seat. "We're going to the playground," I told Jael, who waved an acknowledgement.

On hot summer days when I was little, my father would take me to the playground in Tompkins to cool off in the sprinklers. The smell of water cooking off of asphalt in the sun is one of my strongest sense-memories of childhood. The New York City version of fresh-cut grass, this was the smell of summer. The water from the sprinklers was icy cold, so even though the air was heavy and hot and the sun unforgiving, I could only stay under the frozen shower for a few seconds at a time, running back and forth and shrieking.

He always sat on the closest bench he could without getting wet—close enough to see and hear me, but far enough away that his book wouldn't get splashed. I always tried to get him to come into the water with me, tugging at the cuffs of his jeans, splashing him and giggling, but it never worked. He'd tell me that reading was his favorite game, and he'd rather watch me run.

I considered going to Kmart to buy Riley a bathing suit, but then remembered the change of clothes in her diaper bag. I was in a hurry to get to the sprinklers—I wanted her to understand that I was taking her to do something fun, something that was for her, and didn't want the message to be lost while waiting in a check-out line.

When we arrived at the sprinkler, Riley stopped just outside the water's reach, one hand outstretched toward it. When the freezing drops touched her hand, she pulled it quickly away and looked back at me, disturbed by how cold it was. After I wetted my hand and cooled her forehead with it, she seemed to get the idea. But rather than running in and out like I used to, she just stood there, calculating whether hot or cold was better, wetting one hand at a time, then each foot in turn. She seemed to be having fun in the methodical way that little girls sometimes do.

I parked myself on a bench just beyond the splash zone but close enough that she could see my encouraging nods and smiles. As I wiped the sweat from my face, I considered running through the water, but I took out a book instead. The book I brought with me that day happened to be one of my father's, his name scribbled on the inside of the front cover. I wondered if he had ever read this particular book sitting in this exact spot. If somewhere outside of time we were sitting on this bench, reading this book together.

I looked up at Riley and she was looking at me, her face wrinkled with discomfort, fidgeting her feet in a sort of half-hearted stomp. She didn't know what to do. She reached toward me and grunted—she wasn't talking yet. Remembering how confused I was by my father's stubborn refusal to participate in this summer ritual, I put the book down and kicked off my shoes, the feeling of wet, hot asphalt on bare feet bringing back jolts of memory. I picked her up, her sweaty little body clinging to mine. She wrapped strands of my tangled hair around her grubby fingers and held on a little too tight.

As I ran through the streams of water, I shrieked. She didn't. She was wide-eyed, open-mouthed, shocked by the cold. When we got to the other side, she looked like she might cry. I held my breath, bouncing her a little on my hip. Then she burst into such a giggle fit that she gave herself the hiccups, and started twisting herself out of my arms, reaching back toward the water, ready to go again. I set her down and swung my wet hair off of my face. I was ready to go back to the bench and my book, but she stopped and reached back for my hand.

And then I understood why my father never came into the water: now she expected me to go with her every time. She grinned her gummy grin as I gave her my hand and she wrapped all five of her sticky little fingers around my pointer finger, first pulling me toward the water and then hesitating as the moment came. I gave her a little tug and we ran through—at a toddler's pace, which was slow enough to get us completely soaked. This time she shrieked, too. She wanted me to go with her again, but I shook my head no, encouraging her to go again herself, and retiring gratefully to the bench.

My gaze going back and forth between the pages of my father's book and my happy, giggling goddaughter, I felt my father's presence. In that moment, I understood that there were ways other than staying rooted in mourning to remain connected to him. I could continue our rituals, alone or with Riley, or with my own children someday—but I could grow into the adult role rather than staying stuck as the sad child missing her father. I could remember him on a hot summer day and feel him there with me, rather than only feeling his absence. And I felt the first gentle tugs toward a life that was defined by more than grief.

I wanted to know where the Hunter/Hunted imagery came from, so I went back to Mark, who told me it started at the Loft. In 1983, two years after Cathy died, Joe, Mark, and a few of the people from the New Haven crew signed a ten-year lease for a big abandoned building on Metropolitan Avenue, in Brooklyn. They sanded the floors of what had once been the metalworking factory of Estey Bro.'s Inc., built a kitchen and a bathroom, and put up sheetrock walls to create a practice space for their various bands, a giant living room, and bedrooms large enough to double as studios. Tink was out of high school by then, and she followed.

Another home base for their extended network of transient artists, the Loft, as they dubbed it, was a giant workspace where the artists also lived—as opposed to the Lake Place apartment in New Haven, which had been a party house where artists also worked. At the Loft, the lines between life and art were blurred even more than before; they'd built a lifestyle around their work and a home around that lifestyle. It was the next step in the evolution of Joe's idealized artist life; slightly more mature, more dedicated, more focused.

In order to legally rent the Loft, which was not zoned for residential use, they had to go through a company. So Joe and Mark, who were already doing contracting work here and there, started their own construction company. They named it BB Rodchenko after Russian Constructivist artist Alexander Rodchenko and their own "company names," Biff and Buzzy. BB Rodchenko jobs brought in just enough money for rent and art supplies, and sometimes food. They took small jobs all over the city, painting huge paintings on sheetrock and then sealing them inside of walls—a secret defiance, and a surprise to be discovered during future renovations. There are still buildings in Manhattan and Brooklyn with my father's paintings behind the walls, a secret claim that reminds me the city is mine.

Rodchenko was their favorite Russian Constructivist, but the whole turn-of-the-century movement had a huge impact on the way they thought about art. For the Constructivists, being an artist meant being self-sufficient, capable of creating whatever you might need for survival, and conversant in as many disciplines as possible. Constructivism was less about individual mediums and more about an artist's ability to make use of whatever materials were on hand—and the construction of practical objects as art. It was this concept that drove Joe to make his own sketchbooks and many of his own tools rather than buying them in stores, to repair anything he could avoid replacing.

Everyone at the Loft had a personal live/work space twice the size of a typical New York apartment, and displayed recently completed work in the common space, auditioning for the real world and inviting critique. Years later, when I was a toddler and my father still had his studio in the Loft, he hung my paintings alongside everyone else's on those same walls—the beginning of my (and his) belief that I was not just his child, but another member of this crew of artists, with as much to offer as any of the rest.

Mark remembers that Joe started hoarding more found materials than ever, because the huge Loft space allowed him to collect and collect without running out of space. His room in the Loft had a futon on the floor in one corner, a huge work table in the center, and piles and piles of materials everywhere else. He'd been dragging home huge chunks of scrap metal and fallen branches, and the size of his sculptures grew with the size of his workspace, like a tree finally taken out of a pot and planted in the ground.

Around the beginning of the Loft days, Joe, Mark, and Ken met a guy named Brian Seitz at a gallery opening in Tribeca, and he invited them camping. They went, dubbing themselves the Primitive Hunting Society. Ken explained the rules of the society to me: They had to catch all of their own food in the woods, using only traps and weapons that they made out of trash found on the streets of Brooklyn. They spent a week building up their arsenal (and making elaborate ceremonial headdresses) before heading to the Catskill Mountains.

"The hunting was truly pathetic," Ken told me. "I had focused on collecting screens to catch fish, and I remember telling your dad, 'I've never been laughed at by a fish before.'"

Eventually they admitted defeat. "We decided we'd rather be the Primitive Eating Society," Ken said; they got back in the car and went to buy steaks and whiskey. They kept the original name for future camping trips, but from then on, they brought food and alcohol with them.

The experiment in self-sufficiency may have failed, but the idea of the hunt, the primal thing they had tapped into, that stayed with Joe. It was the next level of what had drawn him to hitchhiking—a pared-down, more essential version of being human.

When they got back to the Loft, he realized that all of those branches he'd been dragging home were just waiting for him to transform them into antlers. He made giant deer-head sculptures out of tree stumps and branches, much bigger than real-life deer. Mythic. He made a herd of deer out of sticks—simple shapes that looked like maybe he'd just tossed a handful of sticks down and they happened to form themselves perfectly into deer with craned necks, well-balanced legs, and majestic antlers. He posed these stick deer in random corners around the Loft, mingling amid guitar cases and amps, grazing on sawdust.

I like that the deer imagery came, at least in part, directly from immersion in nature. I think of my father as so much a creature of the city: gritty and dirty, sullen and snarky, dressed in all black and always ready with a quip. But there was something in him that was wild, too, that wanted the open road and a quiet campsite. Of all the animals in his pantheon, it's deer that feel most like a visit from him when I encounter them in real life.

"Stick Deer:" Carved wood, thorns; 11.5"
(Photographed at the home of Jeff and Lily Joslin, Portland, OR)

I started working harder than ever now that Riley relied on the security of my job and apartment. It began to bother me, though it never had before, that the Apartment was always full of people drinking and being loud. I kept my bedroom door closed to keep out the noise and cigarette smoke, and found that I much preferred reading in bed and listening to Riley's soft sleep noises to drinking and yelling in the living room with my roommates and friends.

I realized just how much I craved real stability—that the freedom to drink beer and smoke cigarettes in my own living room had never been the end of the line. When I first dropped out of high school I'd intended to give myself a break, a chance to breathe, but I figured I'd get back on course eventually. In the four years since, I'd gotten comfortable, living a life that I could have kept living forever: scraping by with shitty jobs, prioritizing time to fuck off and get drunk, wasting away in an aimlessness I told myself was freedom. Riley reminded me to want more.

I started to want a bigger life, but I didn't know where to start. I needed a more drastic change than just taking a few days off of drinking or signing up for a free poetry class somewhere, which had been the extent of my previous attempts at self-improvement. I needed to leave—leave the Apartment, leave my shitty jobs, leave myself. But this felt different from the urge to leave myself that I'd felt before—this time I didn't want obliteration, I wanted escape. I wanted to leave my life behind, but this time I would take myself with me when I went.

I didn't want to leave Riley, but when Jael decided to move in with a new boyfriend in Sunset Park, I took that as a sign and went to California to live with my grandmother Stephanie and my uncle Jake in Marin County for six months. I enrolled at the community college and signed up for an algebra class to prepare for the SATs—plus an astronomy class to get a science credit, and a rigorous ballet intensive to center my brain by strengthening my body for a new start.

I got a job at a consignment store in downtown San Anselmo, and slept on a twin bed in the sun room at the front of my grandmother's house, waking up to the loud, insistent caws of crows and knowing every morning, before I opened my eyes, that I wasn't in Brooklyn anymore. When I got up, Stephanie would have already made coffee, and we would drink it together in the front yard. She had a solid, still calm about her that I always found comforting, and I tried to slow my frenetic internal rhythm to match hers as we breathed in the fresh air of each new day together before I walked the two-and-a-half miles to the College of Marin. The long, solitary walks were the opposite twins of the long walks I used to take in the middle of the night, pacing circles around Manhattan. Now I was walking in the sun, breathing in the smell of wet earth—and I was walking toward something.

I was eighteen years old and hadn't done math homework since I was thirteen, in eighth grade, before we moved back to New York and I decided school was bullshit. The first time I brought a worksheet home to Stephanie's house and sat at the coffee table, trying to solve equations that my brain could barely follow, I wanted to give up after ten minutes. I didn't know how to do algebra. I didn't belong in school. This whole thing was a bad idea…and this was exactly why I'd needed to leave my regular life to do this—if I'd been back at the Apartment, I would have just thrown the stupid worksheet away and gone out to the living room to have a beer, writing the whole school thing off as a failed experiment. But now I was in California, with nothing to do but try again. By the end of the semester I had gotten my GED through the community college, a decent enough score on the SATs, and a transcript full of A's to balance out the one from Bard that was all F's. And I was sticking perfect triple pirouettes when I'd only ever been able to do singles before, laughing every time I landed and found myself facing the right direction.

Jake and Stephanie and I took a walk in the woods one day, and stopped to take a break on a big rock. We were still and quiet enough that a huge buck with majestic antlers didn't seem to notice us when he stopped a few yards away to nibble some grass. When he finally realized we were there, he lifted his head and stared directly at me. We held eye contact for what felt like several minutes, and I could feel the heat rising in my cheeks as my eyes filled with tears. I felt like I was shedding a thousand heavy layers, almost ready to spring forward into newness, and I felt sure that this deer was a message from my father, urging me on. When he finally bounded away, it felt like a demonstration of how to move unimpeded, light and quick and sure.

Before I flew home, I wrote an impassioned letter to the admissions committee at the New School, explaining that I'd dropped out of high school because I couldn't trust my education in the reckless hands of the New York City public school system, and including a long list of everything I'd read in the years between Bard and Marin—histories of the labor movement in New York, the great Russian and American classics, way more Shakespeare than I would have read in high school, the Beats, my father's books of art theory and poetry. I'd kept myself busy, I explained, developing a work ethic by waiting tables since I was fourteen and moving out of my mother's apartment at sixteen; enriching my mind by taking figure drawing classes at the Art Students' League and ballet at Third Street and Joffrey, and having long, passionate conversations with the city's intellectual underbelly. I left out the fact that I spent as much time tripping on acid at Rockaway Beach as I did practicing ballet, that when I moved out of my mother's apartment it was into a flop-house in Bed-Stuy that eventually housed five other teenagers and a baby, and that many of my most stimulating political and artistic debates were with my fellow drop-outs and the freaks I ran into wandering the streets in the middle of the night.

They bought it.

Carved wood, scrap metal hinges; 35″
(Photographed at the home of
Heidi O'Donnell, Phoenicia, NY)

Opposite page: Carved, painted, and burned wood; approx. 36" (Photographed at the home of Joni Wehrli, NYC)

Carved wood with existing construction markings; 33" (Photographed at the home of Heidi O'Donnell, Phoenicia, NY)

Carved wood and lacquered bark; 8″
(Photographed at the home of Heidi O'Donnell, Phoenicia, NY)

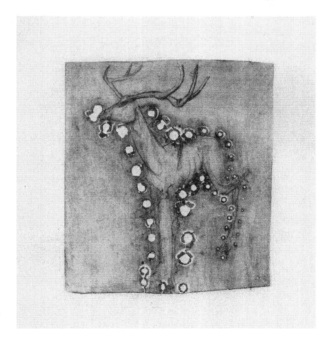

Top: "Aim:" Woodcut on paper
(Note: A copy of this print hangs in Josie's bar, a gift from the author)

Bottom: Etching, drawing, and burned holes on paper

Top: Woodcut and leaf print on paper

Bottom: Woodcut and leaf pochoir on layered paper

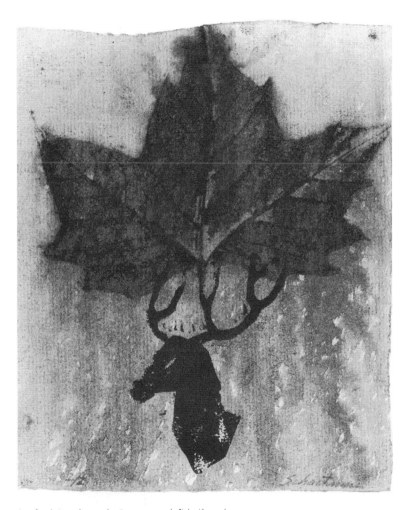

Leaf print and woodcut on paper, left in the rain

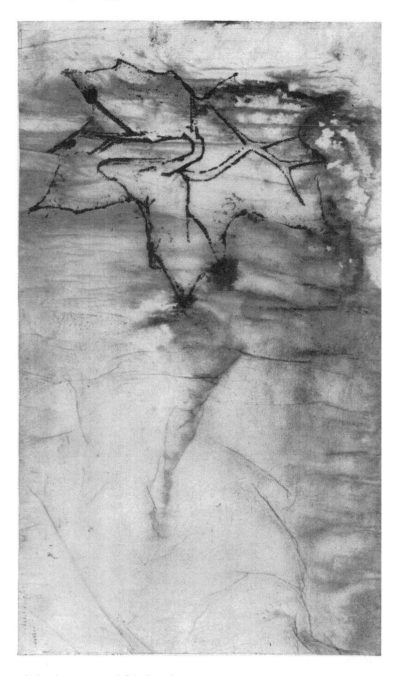

Ink drawing on paper, left in the rain

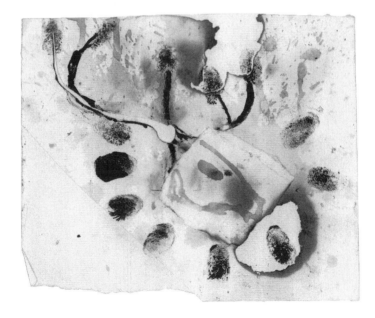

Top: Woodcut on paper

Bottom: Ink drawing, fingerprints, and berry juice on burned paper

Woodcut on paper

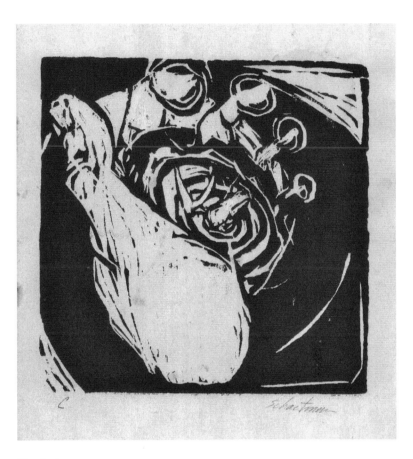

Woodcut on paper

When I first started at the New School, I felt distinctly, completely separate from my classmates. I'd worked a dozen different jobs to support myself and begged on the street for change to fill the gaps. I'd drunk enough vodka that the smell of it still makes me sick to this day and switched to whiskey, taken enough hallucinogens that the magic wore off, developed and kicked a coke habit. I'd been reading fiction and poetry, philosophy and history and literary criticism all along, but by the time I started college I was thirsty for someone to tell me what to make of it all, and ready to get serious. Most of my classmates were living away from home for the first time, having never worked a day in their lives—or maybe a summer job at most—and were more excited about dorm life and the wonders of their very first alcoholic beverages than they were about the rigor and structure of academia. I felt about ten years older than them, and worlds apart.

Jael and I fell into something like a divorced-parents' routine: me taking Riley for a night or two once in a while, or just for a day, to take her to the sprinkler park, the toy store, the Polish diner. The first time she stayed over with me at my new place when she was three or four—I'd just moved in with Leah on Avenue A—I was nervous about her falling off of my loft bed. I put her on the inside and slept on the outside edge, curled around her, my body a buffer. I told her before we went to sleep, "This is really important. I don't want you trying to get down by yourself, ok? Wake me up as soon as you wake up in the morning, and we'll get down together, ok?" She agreed, and woke me at dawn, earnest and pleased with herself for following the rules. I thanked her, helped her down the ladder, and we were at Neptune eating pancakes before the sun was fully up, spending as much of the day together as possible before I brought her back to her mom. We went on like this for a few years until they moved up to Ithaca, and then I saw her once or twice a year. I understood a little better then what it must have been like for my father when my mother and I moved to Carmel; I was happy for Riley, knew Ithaca would be a great place for her to grow up, surrounded by trees and Jael not struggling as hard to scrape by. But I missed being able to see her whenever I had a free afternoon.

I was working at Sidewalk Cafe on Avenue A, and worked my way up from server to cocktail server to bartender over the course of my first two years at the New School. I was eager to get behind the bar because the money was better, and because it put physical space between me and the customers, but mostly because it meant a set schedule. Server schedules were determined by the manager each week, and no matter how many times I blocked off my class times on the request sheet, I could never quite get all of them off and constantly had to choose between skipping class and missing a shift. Every time I had to do the math of how many absences I could have before my grades suffered and how many shifts I could miss before I'd be short on rent, it was hard not to resent the fact that most of my classmates didn't have to work at all, rent checks from their parents delivered every month as if by some grown-up tooth fairy.

My mother joked once that she had actually helped me pay for college by being so poor that I qualified for the maximum amount of federal financial aid. I could barely fake a smile as I thought about how hard it had been to get that financial aid when I couldn't prove my mother's income because she hadn't filed taxes in years—and because she basically didn't have any. I remembered crying in the financial aid office and insisting, "She hasn't paid my bills since I was fifteen years old. Can I just bring you a signed letter saying that?" and demanding, "What would you do if I didn't have a relationship with her at all? What do you do when kids are estranged from their parents?" and getting an unsympathetic, bureaucratic shrug in response.

Standing in that office, all the frustration of being a poor kid at a rich kid school, all the built-up desire for help and support that you have to repress when your whole sense of identity is based on being a scrapper who can take care of herself, all the exhaustion from pushing myself beyond my physical limits to make it to work and class and sometimes straight back to work again without so much as a nap in between, came pouring out. I sunk down to the carpeted floor, cross-legged, tear-stained, sniffling, and refused to leave until they made some phone calls and found someone to explain the options for applying for financial aid without a parent's tax returns. Eventually they agreed to accept copies of her bank statements and verification that she received disability benefits from the state, and I couldn't stop myself from asking "Was that so fucking hard?" before standing up and walking out with my chin high as if I hadn't just groveled.

I was determined to pass for a well-adjusted young adult among my new peers at school, even if I didn't interact with them much. I was starting fresh, or playing dress-up; I wasn't sure which. But either way, it felt like a high-stakes game to see if I could slip in among them undetected. I cut my long, scraggly hair to above my chin like a '20s flapper and dyed it bright blonde. I wore pencil skirts down to my knees with lace-up Oxford heels and vintage silk blouses—I had no idea how to dress like a normal person after years of ripped fishnets and combat boots, so I just decided to dress like I was going to an office job in the '70s and see if that worked.

I went to Red Hook every Wednesday night to watch my old friends from the park play folk music at a music school/theater next to the highway. After the show ended we'd pull the gate down over the window of the bar next door and drink and smoke until dawn, and I felt like I still belonged somewhere—like I could stop projecting the image I kept up for the rest of the week. I'd gone out of my way as a teenager to make sure nobody ever mistook me for a college student—college students were gentrifier larvae; that was how the transplants got here, and then they stayed and ruined everything with the trendy coffee shops and brunch restaurants that catered to them pushing out the local businesses that made New York neighborhoods special. I still didn't want to be one of them, even if I kind of was.

But then one day in Intro to Journalism, someone said something insufferably stupid, and I made an involuntary face of disgust. I heard the tiniest little stifled laugh and looked across the table to see the sweet Texan girl who always sat there meeting my eyes with a mischievous smile. After that, whenever someone said something ignorant or way off base I would look up at Carly and we'd both roll our eyes and snicker. We had whole conversations with our facial expressions, so that the first time we went out for coffee after class, we already had the rhythm of close friends. She was cheerful and clean-cut and everything I wasn't, but there was a sharp wit underneath her shiny surface that I recognized, something I saw in her that saw me back.

We were both intrigued and a little intimidated by the student newspaper, the *New School Free Press*, and agreed we'd join together. The first day, we sat together in the middle of the second row of chairs with built-in desk flaps. As we watched the student editors up at the front of the room, running the show, cracking jokes with each other but being serious about the work they expected us all to do, Carly and I agreed in hushed whispers that we would be up there by the following year.

After years of cultivated apathy, I poured all of my repressed caring into the newspaper. We knew nobody read it, but that didn't matter.

We worked like we were producing the only source of news for a community that needed it, with the idealism and grave seriousness of student journalists not yet worn out with years of working in a broken industry.

Most of the stories were small, insignificant even to the community they served. But once in a while we got a big one, like a piece I worked on for months with another student reporter about how the New School wasn't accurately reporting sexual assault statistics as required by federal law; or the student occupation, a precursor to the Occupy Wall Street protests, which we covered around the clock.

I started spending all of my time with the newspaper crew. We stayed late every day in our office on the fourth floor, debating story placement and headline phrasing until the custodians kicked us out. Then we dragged ourselves to the bar around the corner from school, rowdy with exhaustion and satisfaction, riffing on puns we'd made earlier in the day and taking turns buying pitchers of beer.

Now that I was bartending at night—first at Sidewalk and then at Sophie's on Fifth Street—I didn't have to play the un-winnable Tetris of lining up my ever-changing waitressing schedule with my classes. I didn't sign up for any early morning classes on days following my bar shifts, and managed to work out a livable routine that allowed for at least a few hours of sleep every night. I signed up for writing classes in every genre, literature classes to fill the gaps of my self-directed "home schooling," and a ballet class.

My grades went up, and I tried to focus less on the ways I was different from my classmates and just let myself be a kid in college, with friends. I learned to let the scowl fall away from my face. We went out drinking and I learned to just have a couple of beers instead of turning every evening into a competition with myself to see how many shots I could throw back. A group of us went to Long Island for a long weekend, lounging in the sun reading back issues of *The New Yorker* and drinking frozen margaritas we'd made with berries from the farm stand down the road. Slowly, bit by bit, normal and happy felt less and less like an act.

But as I let myself become this new person, I felt my old self, the self who had a father and then even the self who mourned my father, falling away. I felt adulthood pulling me forward, and I wondered where and how my father would fit into my life then. I wondered if he would even know me now, if I was abandoning him by letting myself enjoy a life that he wasn't part of and wouldn't recognize—that he might even sneer at and call bougie.

So much about my life was different now, but one of the hardest things to adjust to was the fact that I was meeting all these new people who didn't know that my father was dead, that there was a huge smoking crater in the center of my life. Even when I told them, it came out like any other piece of biographical information, like the fact that I did spelling bees as a kid. When I was a teenager and people heard that my father was dead, they understood how wrong that was, how much I must hurt. But now I was an adult, and adults exist without their parents, so nobody seemed to understand the weight of his absence.

So I read his notebooks, finally, after so many years of carrying them around like a secret, looking for a new connection to him. That night, as I scoured my father's notebooks for something to keep me tethered to him, pulling his leather jacket tight around my body, I didn't know I was starting what would become a years-long search.

Shortly after the night when I read my father's notebooks and realized that his artwork was where he'd left himself behind for me, I had a vivid nightmare. I was in a Salvation Army-like thrift store, and I wandered over to the dishware-and-knick-knacks section. I saw a bunch of my father's smaller sculptures on a tall shelf amid mismatched plates and stopped clocks, for sale for a few dollars each. I panicked in the dream, screaming to everyone and to no one in particular, "These are mine!" When I woke up with that same desperate feeling of *These are mine!* sitting in my chest, I realized it had always been there.

My father was transient during the last few years of his life, crashing with one friend or another for a few weeks or a few months before moving on and leaving the pile of new work he'd created behind "for safe keeping," though he never went back for any of it. Whenever he needed money, which was all the time between the child support he was always behind on and the heroin habit that needed constant maintenance, he would call up old friends and see if anyone wanted to buy one of the pieces he'd managed to hold onto.

Whenever I thought of my father's work scattered across the country, sold, given away, or abandoned during hasty moves with no clear destination, I felt the same tightness in my chest as I did in the Salvation Army dream. I still do. Even about the pieces I know are cherished by his closest friends. It's an anxiety that goes beyond logical concern for the preservation of his art and becomes a frantic, pressing need to claim and hoard every scrap of what's left of him.

I started fantasizing about driving around the country with a U-Haul to collect the work he left "for safe keeping." I wanted to surround myself with it, dog masks and deer peeping out from every corner, prints piled everywhere like a hoarder's old newspapers. And I started trying to think of the least morbid way to ask everyone who has any of his work that they don't want to part with now to please stipulate in their wills that it go to me when they die. I was filled with terror at the possibility that, when his friends die, whoever is tasked with cleaning out their homes might not understand that the slightly dilapidated and mildly creepy art on the walls is my birthright. They might put these precious artifacts in storage to rot, throw them away, or donate them and bring my nightmare to life.

Becoming increasingly desperate as I thought about the urgency of this need to collect, I mentioned something to my mother over the phone about my plan to start attempting to consolidate my father's work, or at the very least photograph it for my book project and an archive. She agreed, "We should definitely do that." I balked. I had never said anything about "we." (*These are* mine!)

This was something I had to do myself, I stumbled to explain; my father's work is my legacy and it really didn't have anything to do with her, his ex-wife. She pushed back, offended, feeling excluded, not understanding why we couldn't just do it together. Like Hercules' mother wanting to help him fight the lion.

"If he'd had a will," I said through clenched teeth, "you wouldn't have been in it." I was angry, resorting to a reminder that they hated each other for the last several years of his life.

"That's not the point!" she yelled, starting to cry. I was silent on the other end of the line, waiting for her to collect herself, willing myself not to say anything even more cruel.

Finally, calmer, she said, "You know, even when things were bad with us, there was part of me that always thought we'd still end up together." She wanted me to understand why she felt like it was her legacy, too. But the harder she pushed, the more I shut down. I'd felt so cut off from her for so long, it was too late to become a "we" now that she wanted in on something that felt so clearly mine.

All of the hardness I've felt toward her in my life started with my parents splitting up. I was seven, and all I knew about what happened was that my mother took me and left my father behind. I knew that she made him cry. I didn't know why she left, I just knew that it was her decision to end our family, and then, soon after, her decision to move us to Carmel to live with her new boyfriend in a big empty house so that my father was a three-hour bus ride away. She was clearly the villain in this story.

These days, she calls him her great love, talks about him like his death is the only reason they're not together. But every time she plays the grieving widow role, posting on Facebook about how handsome he was and how much she misses him, my angry child voice screams in my mind, "You left him!" I remember a broken home, and when it feels like she doesn't, I want to rage at her and snatch back the grief that, in those moments, I'm convinced she has no right to claim.

I was afraid to let her into this project—afraid her emotion would drown me like when we wrote those letters to each other in Fort Ord, my little offering of grief swept away by the tsunami of my mother. And I was afraid to let her in because it was mine: I was piecing together my father's story, I was conjuring him, I was writing the response to the call of his artwork. I was afraid that this story about my father would become the story of her lost love.

But I also knew I couldn't do this without her. Their love was a major part of his story—he was in love with her for a quarter of the time he was alive. She was his wife, the mother of his child. I knew she would have by far the most to tell me about who my father really was—what it was like to make a life with him, what he worried about and talked about and dreamed of in the quiet moments. She would know when he was making what and how he balanced the artist's life with a family, and she would know when he was using and when he was clean. So of course I had to make room here for my mother's memories, and even her emotions. Still, the role reversal felt strange when I found myself, for maybe the first time ever, asking my mother to tell me more about her feelings.

On May 14, 1987, Joe and Mark walked into Billy's Topless Bar on Sixth Avenue and 23rd Street. It was a Thursday, and it would've been Cathy's thirtieth birthday if she hadn't died six years earlier. They had probably come from a construction job, covered in plaster and paint as usual, looking to distract my father from the sad anniversary with booze and naked women.

My mother remembers this night, the night they met, like a scene from a movie she's watched a hundred times. Sitting on the floor of my tiny East Village bedroom, I poured her a glass of cheap wine and asked her to tell me the story, though I'd heard it enough times to recite it myself.

Heidi—my mother—was on stage dancing and, as she tells it, she and Joe locked eyes the moment the guys walked in the door. He was lean but muscular, with an exaggerated slouch and the leather-jacket-and-black-jeans uniform of the New York art scene. At first though, all she saw was his face—his pale blue eyes and what she describes as the mischief that was always on his lips.

She looked like a comic book rendition of the stripper dream girl; simultaneously angular and voluptuous, sweet apple cheeks under dark eyes, with cropped black hair and a reckless attitude that made it believable when she claimed, years later, that Mia Wallace from *Pulp Fiction* had been based on her.

Mark, standing behind Joe, not even able to see the look on his face, said, *There's the girl for you.*

That night at Billy's, for once in the history of strip clubs, it wasn't just the customer staring; she stared right back at him. The dancers spent every other half-hour offstage, talking to customers, and Heidi spent all of her floor time with Joe.

He stayed for her whole shift, until four in the morning, and then took her back in a cab to her friend Hannah's apartment on Ludlow Street, where she was staying—the same apartment Hannah lived in when my mother and I returned to New York, the same block as Hannah's vintage store that my mother and I slept in the back room of that first month back in the city, and where we shared a studio apartment after that. They stood on the street corner, kissing and saying long goodbyes. Back then, the intersection of Ludlow and Houston was deserted late at night, so they were alone under the towering parking structure on the corner, under yellow streetlights and a hazy New York City late spring pre-dawn sky. I closed my eyes and imagined that night, the love story that created and scarred my life starting on a street corner that I passed thousands of times. I pictured myself, an angry drunk teenager clomping down the street in my combat boots, walking past the ghost of that first kiss.

"He didn't come inside, but we didn't know how to leave each other," my mother told me. "It was weird since we'd just met that night. We didn't know if we'd ever see each other again, but it was like we'd die if we didn't."

She wasn't even supposed to be at Billy's that night, she said, hinting at fate. She was covering a shift for Hannah, who wanted the night off. Not only was it not her regular shift, it was her first shift ever. Heidi had arrived from Buffalo just a few days earlier to visit Hannah, a short visit that turned into six years.

Part of my mother's childhood was spent dirt poor on a farm, living off the edible weeds she could forage in the woods—poor like you picture the dustbowl, the Great Depression, but this was the 1970s in West Virginia. Before that she'd been in a nightmare of a foster home with rationed toilet paper and abundant, malicious terror. She'd lived through things that would make some people hard, but she didn't come out weathered and tough, she came out fragile, frozen in the innocence upon which that torment had been inflicted. There is something about her to this day that gives the impression that she's still the five-year-old who found herself suddenly without her mother, in a cruel stranger's home. She's still the nine-year-old picking wild lemongrass for her and her sisters to share for lunch. If I can still see that scared little girl in her eyes now, I can only imagine the tenderness of the wide-eyed twenty-year-old who arrived in New York.

"I stepped out of the cab on First and First—which I was very confused by—and into a ridiculous world of experience that completely altered the course of my life," she said, making a big gesture with her glass that almost spilled wine everywhere.

That summer, a heat wave coincided with a garbage strike in New York, and the whole city smelled like baking, putrefied trash. Joe and Heidi were so giddily in love that they barely noticed, taking walks around the city and eating Klondike bars in Union Square. They were both already doing heroin when they met, but she says he didn't like to do it with her—maybe a reticence left over from his experience with Cathy.

Through all of this, my father was still in a relationship with Tink after seven dysfunctional years. Heidi knew about Tink, but Tink didn't know about Heidi.

After years of dogs and deer, the female form began to dominate my father's art. More specifically, he started drawing and sculpting Heidi's body. He had drawn women before, in figure-drawing classes as a teenager and at art school, and then when Cathy made occasional appearances in the work they did together. But in those paintings, Cathy's body was one of many parts of the graphic image, weighted equally with the drape of the kimono she wore or the dogs she shared the canvas with. The women in those paintings happened to look like Cathy because she was there to model, just like his drawings of hands always look like his own because they were the easiest to reference. These new pieces were not just of Heidi but *about* her, her physicality, her sexuality, and the hold she had on him. He often drew and sculpted her as Daphne—the nymph from Greek myth who transformed into a tree to escape an aggressive suitor. The beautiful woman not quite attainable. The most iconic of his Daphne sculptures—a woman's torso that is unmistakably my mother's, carved out of a branch with the bark still on either end, as if the sculpture itself was caught mid-transformation—lives in my mother's living room, along with a Daphne that my father drew on the back of her Barbizon Modeling School certificate.

The drawing is a clear precursor to the Daphne that was tattooed on my mother's arm a few years later, with purple and green roots winding around her bicep and willow branches draped over her shoulder. I was there when she got it done, and I remember the basement apartment where her friend Ranelle's boyfriend Jay tattooed her while I played with their cat and drew a big abstract mixed media piece with nail polish and crayon. It was 1991 and tattooing was still illegal in New York City, so it was always done like this—hidden, secret, illicit. The tattoo was never finished because, my mom says, Jay was so strung out that he started nodding off while tattooing the purple roots. Some of the lines are blurry and thicker than they're supposed to be, but she never got it fixed. It's faded now, some of the light green leaves barely visible. It's the image I had in mind when I started getting my own tattoos twenty years later, wishing they would look as soft and faded as my mother's right away, impatient with their brightness.

I was three years old and a tattoo gun didn't stand out to me as any different from other art supplies I saw every day. It was louder than a paint brush but not louder than a band saw. Skin as canvas was new though, and I watched, fascinated, as the tree woman appeared on my tree mother's arm, like I watched her put her makeup on in the morning. I watched her create herself—blow-drying her hair so she was surrounded in warmth, lining her eyes with black, dabbing little bits of sweet, musky-smelling amber resin on her neck, lacing up tall patent leather boots—just as intently as I watched my father create his odes to her out of wood and glass and metal. The tattoo was one more form of art-making and one more form of woman-making.

As my mother and I talked about the Daphne sculptures and her tattoo, I remembered how in awe I was of her when I was very young. I remembered that other version of her: magical tree woman, my witchy, sparkly-eyed Mama so much prettier and more special than any other mama, before she became the weepy adversary that I constantly braced against. And I remembered that while I'd aligned myself with my father for so long, the first thing I ever had in common with him was how much we both loved my mother.

"Daphne:" Carved wood; 20"
(Photographed at the home of
Heidi O'Donnell, Phoenicia, NY)

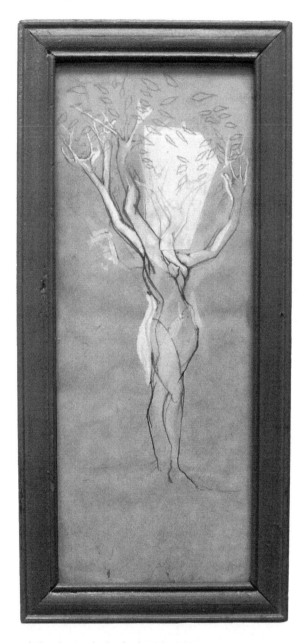

Ink drawing on the back of Heidi's Barbizon
Modeling School certificate of completion.
Green leaves painted on the inside of the glass frame

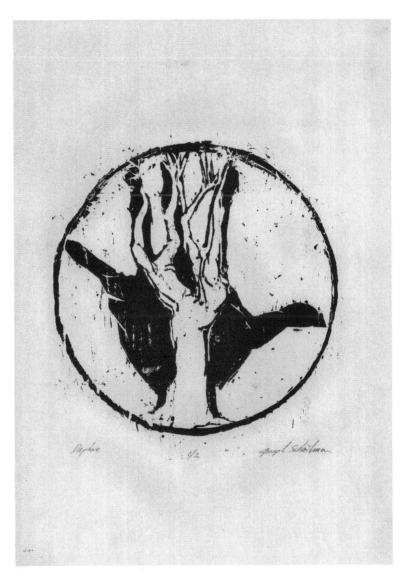

"Daphne:" Woodcut on paper

Pink lipstick kiss (Heidi's) and woodcut on paper

When I was very little, my mother told me I was conceived in the woods, a fairy child.

In late August of 1987, a few months after Joe and Heidi met, she went with him to Mount Baldy in Mendocino County, California for a job insulating a tiny cabin. She refers to it as their love nest, the first time they got to be together every day and feel like a real couple, not sneaking around behind Tink's back—just being together in nature and in love. An entry in her diary from that time describes it as "divine, and sweet as hell."

After the job was over, he went back to the Loft in Brooklyn and she stayed in San Francisco to visit friends. A few weeks after he left, she realized she was pregnant, and told him over the phone.

Sitting in my bedroom, two decades after that phone call, she hesitated at this point in the story, where we both knew the fairy-tale-love-story part was over and it was about to get messy. I refilled her wine glass and reassured her that I knew my father had made some mistakes, that this whole exercise would be pointless if I didn't hear the whole story. I'd heard bits and pieces of what came next plenty of times, and promised her I wouldn't be destroyed by a few more details.

"He wasn't mean or awful about it," she began, still hedging, trying to defend his memory, entreating me with her eyes to understand, "but he wanted me to have an abortion."

She said it like she expected it to break my heart, with a tenderness that annoyed me—her head down, eyes peeking up at me from under her bangs. I looked inside myself for a part that was hurt by the fact that my father wanted me aborted, but I couldn't find one. Of course he did. He didn't know it was me, it was just an abstract idea of a baby, an impediment to his lifestyle, a responsibility he didn't want. He was older than my mother, thirty years to her 21, but a thirty-year-old who lived in an abandoned factory and liked to hitchhike and made art out of roadkill. Not exactly stable fatherhood material.

Not even sure at the time if she meant it, she told him that she'd raise their child alone if she had to, but she was going to keep it. While they were deciding what to do, she flew back to New York and back to Billy's, dancing as much as she could before her belly started to grow— she'd need money if she was about to become a single mother.

Now that there was tangible, living evidence of their affair, Joe told Tink about Heidi and about the pregnancy.

"I was on stage at Billy's one day and Tink came in," my mother told me. "And sat, and cried." Tink didn't say anything. She just came to see her, to see what she looked like and try to believe that she was real. I pictured Tink, walking into Billy's in the middle of the day shift with her short, boyish hair and her army jacket. Back-lit, standing in the doorway, eyes adjusting to the smoky darkness and catching the reflections on the mirrored walls and the silver poles. Some cheesy '80s strip-bar song blasting from the juke—"Pour Some Sugar on Me" came out that year, 1987; imagine how many times it played in strip joints that fall. How did she know which one was Heidi? Had someone shown her a picture? Did she just know, in that way that women do? Was Heidi showing yet, a tiny little baby bump that customers wouldn't notice, but that Tink knew to look for?

Heidi, by several accounts, looked a lot like Cathy (Ken said it was like *Vertigo*). I don't see it. But then, she's my mother and I know her face too well to mistake it for a long-dead Germanic beauty who exists only in photographs. But to Tink, staring at the stripper who was pregnant with her always-unattainable boyfriend's child, Heidi looked just like Cathy—which, Tink told me, she was not surprised by. For their whole relationship up to that point, Tink had been second in line to a dead woman. Now she'd been replaced by a new, living woman who was more like the dead woman than she'd ever been.

Who felt worse in that moment: Tink, sitting there comparing herself to this gorgeous, sexy, half-naked woman on stage who she knew was filling the role she'd never been able to—or Heidi, on stage, exposed, nowhere to run, dancing in her underwear while this girl she'd helped betray sat in front of her and cried?

Even after that, somehow, Joe and Tink didn't break up. Their relationship had been security for him all along, and so it stayed. As long as he was with her, he had the option of pretending nothing had changed, of running back to the Loft where he was making art all day, every day, and selling some of it. She was his tether to this life where nothing was demanded of him—the opposite of his relationship with Heidi, which was sweeping him away, making him care deeply about something other than his art and threatening to change everything forever.

During this period, Joe started the Bad Barbie series, small statue-like sculptures—most around eight inches tall, but some shorter, and some close to two feet. They're female forms, but just the torso, and legs that join together into a sharp spike. They don't have arms or heads, but many have ponytails of human hair—many of them Heidi's. Once word was out that he was always looking for hair as material, friends and friends of friends would save their ponytails for him when they cut their hair, girls handing them off to Heidi in the strip-club dressing room like something illicit. Some of the Bad Barbies are cast in silicone, with hair or feathers or anything else suspended inside. Some are cast in lead. Many incorporate animal bones and found metal or glass fragments, concrete, rubber. They were the richest ground yet for his experimentation with materials.

"The Barbies couldn't run, their legs were these spikes, jammed into wood, but was it that they were trapped or that they were dangerous?" my mother asked, talking to me but also asking herself and also maybe asking my father. *Are they hunting or hunted?*

I once asked my father to make a Bad Barbie with my hair, not understanding that they were dark or sexual, just that they were pretty. He obliged, always willing to include me, but he made it tiny, out of clear silicone, with one bright blonde curl; the purest-looking one in the series.

"They were these intense, sexy, dangerous creatures," my mother said. "They were obviously pretty dark but they were also celebratory. I saw more mysterious sexual tension in them than just darkness." They may be trapped and/or dangerous, but they're also beautiful, with carefully crafted hips, stomachs, and breasts. They're the visceral, raw, jagged side of femininity. A kind of snarling womanhood that I inherited both from my mother and from growing up surrounded by these sculptures made in her image.

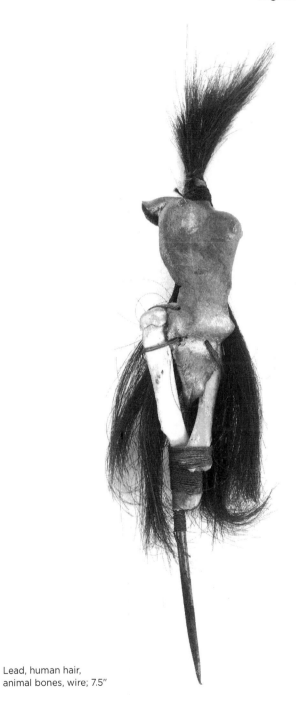

Lead, human hair,
animal bones, wire; 7.5″

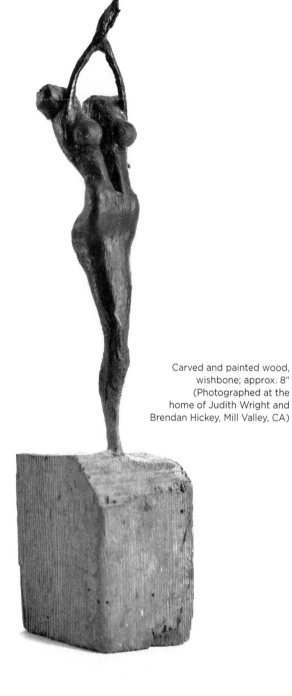

Carved and painted wood,
wishbone; approx. 8″
(Photographed at the
home of Judith Wright and
Brendan Hickey, Mill Valley, CA)

Lead, human hair,
animal bones; approx. 9″

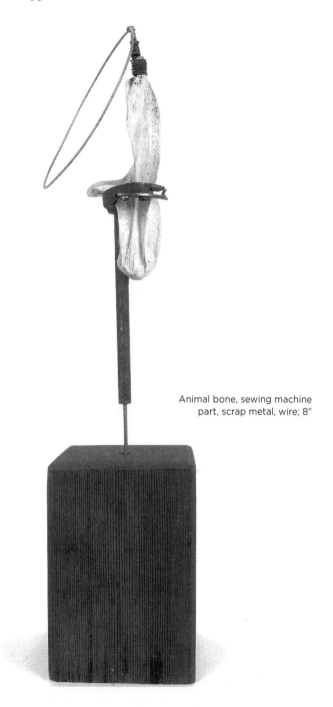

Animal bone, sewing machine
part, scrap metal, wire; 8″

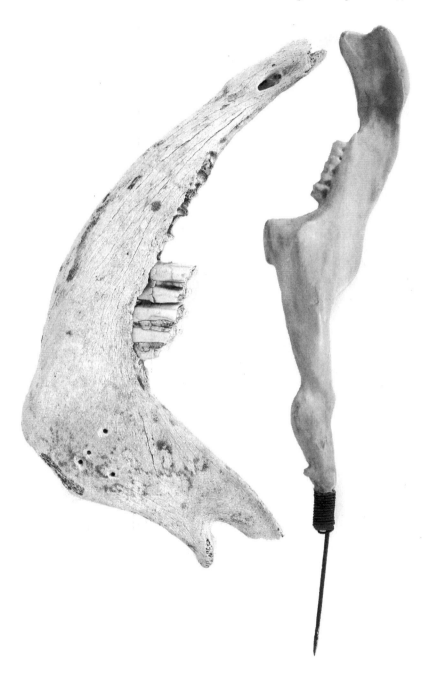

Jaw bones, one carved and one untouched

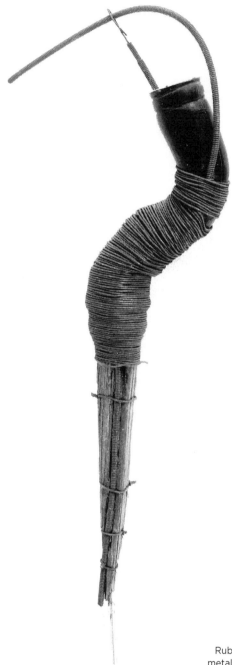

Rubber tubing, scrap
metal, copper wire; 16"

Lead, human hair,
Slinky; approx. 14″

Human hair, sparrow
wings; approx. 18″

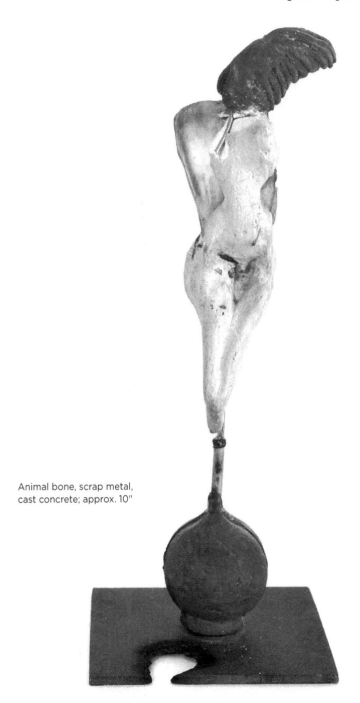

Animal bone, scrap metal,
cast concrete; approx. 10″

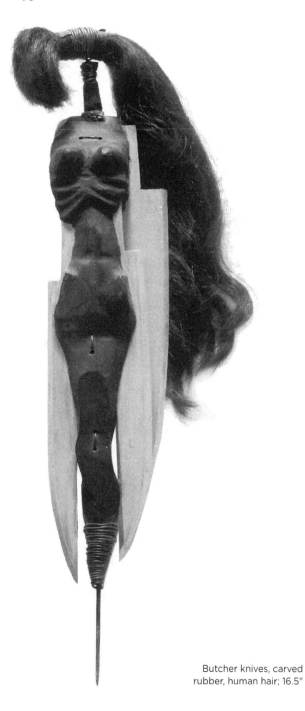

Butcher knives, carved
rubber, human hair; 16.5"

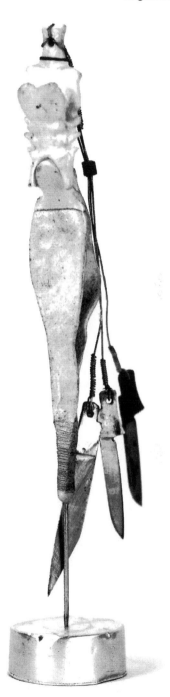

Animal bones, pocket knife blades, wire; approx. 6″ (Photographed at the home of Stephanie and Jake O'Donnell, San Anselmo, CA)

Still not knowing whether he was going to step up and not willing to stay in New York, pregnant and alone while she waited for him to decide, Heidi went back to Buffalo to be near her mother, Stephanie, who was also pregnant at the time—with my uncle Jake.

Joe and Heidi each visited each other once during the pregnancy, and wrote lots of letters. He flip-flopped frantically between panicked cruelty and romantic grandeur. In one letter he wrote that it wouldn't be healthy for them to continue as "lovers" because he would always wonder if he was with her for the baby's sake. Then in another he dismissed all of his own fears, writing, "fuck that, remember the future?"

He was certain that it was a bad idea for him to be a father. But somehow he wanted to do it anyway, and that scared the crap out of him.

After our first interview, my mother left a big stack of these letters for me to read and decipher, all on different sizes and colors of paper, many torn, folded, stained—a record of the creation of our family. She placed the stack in my outstretched hands and held on for a beat before she relinquished them. I felt their weight, figurative and literal. She made me promise I'd give them back, and I thought about whether I would ever hand over my love letters to anyone, even my own child. I don't think I would. I thought about how she could have said no, but I knew she never would, willing to give me any and all of herself. For a moment, I loved her simply and without reservation.

She came back to my apartment again a few months later, when I'd read all the letters, pieced together their love and his doubt and her rage and fear. Again, we sat on the floor. I gave her a pillow to sit on because last time her back hurt when she left. I poured wine and laid the letters out on the floor, in piles, where I'd sorted them into categories: *love letters from him, love letters from her, mean letters from him, angry letters from her.* Although I'd read all about it, I still wanted to hear the story from her, from the now version of her. I asked what it was like to be pregnant and not know whether he was going to stick around.

I always knew that she was a young mother, but that's an abstract concept to a child. Sitting there talking about her pregnancy, I was exactly the same age she had been then. Twenty-one years old barely felt like adulthood to me. I was still in school, just deciding who I wanted to be. When she was that age, she was pregnant and alone. I understood in a way that I never had before how terrified she must have been. I understood what she'd meant all the times she told me "I was just a kid," by way of explaining her mistakes in mothering.

"When we were near each other, he was suddenly wonderful," she said. "Then he'd leave and send me a terrible letter. Then he'd send me a nice letter. It was torturing me."

She began to lose patience with him. One letter she wrote in February of 1988, when she was five months pregnant, opens with, "I think your [sic] one of the biggest cowards I've ever known—maybe the biggest. I hate you."

Telling me this story years later, she was much more forgiving. She laced descriptions of her own anger and misery with explanations of how scared and confused he was.

"He never wanted to have kids," she said. "He thought he'd be a very bad father." I knew from conversations I had with him when I was a child that he lived in fear of taking after his own harsh and overbearing father. He would tell me, "I won't make you do anything you don't want to, that's what my father did with me and I want to be better."

Barry Schactman—my grandfather, whose friends called him Bobby—was a painter and an art professor at Washington University in St. Louis. A fastidious, sharp man, he was a strict, unforgiving teacher, rumored to have made students cry on a regular basis and to have never given anyone an "A" in his decades-long career. At home, Joe and his little sister Amy referred to their father as "Moses" because of how important rules were to him.

I found out by searching through public documents online that my grandfather was in the Army before he settled into the ivory tower. I don't know why nobody ever told me this before—it never came up in any of my father's tales of his father's rigidity, though it would have fit. Barry wanted everything to be just so, and his wife Phyllis Rita played her part by marking the floor with tape where the chair legs were supposed to go.

Barry made his career with large-scale paintings of Holocaust victims, dead or dying, emaciated, writhing in torment. He spent decades sequestered in his studio, a high-ceilinged addition he'd had built onto the house. I saw it once, and I remember it feeling cavernous despite its many huge windows. Sometimes he wouldn't come out for meals, and it was understood that it wasn't because he'd forgotten, which meant he wasn't to be reminded. Over and over, for years and years, he painted the dead and dying piled on top of each other in slightly different positions: this time looking straight out at the viewer, as if pleading for help, this time with all of their faces obscured, this time calling out toward the sky.

He enrolled his son in university-level drawing classes when he was a freshman in high school. "Our dad was supportive of his artwork, always inspiring him and showing him and helping him," Amy told me. "But as soon as your Papa began to find his own vision, style, expression, my father was just judgmental and critical. He looked down upon any art that deviated from classical and technical." And of course he didn't take kindly to his son dropping out of art school.

Barry was also a former boxer, and Amy remembers him "beating the shit out of [her] brother" a couple of times.

One of my earliest memories is of walking with my father past a tall chain-link fence, on one of those winter days when the sun is so bright in the crisp, cold air that everything looks stark and white like an over-exposed photograph. I was just learning to talk and still wobbling when I walked, maybe two years old. I remember staring at the shadow the fence created on the sidewalk. As we walked together I held onto his pointer-and-middle fingers in my fist—that was how we held hands when I was little, his alternative to enveloping all of my tiny fingers in his calloused hand. Trying to get his attention, maybe to ask him about the shadows, I tugged at his fingers and said some variation of "Daddy" or "Dad."

He stopped walking. It was cold enough that I could see my breath as he stood still, deciding what exactly to say. He was backlit, a big looming silhouette. He looked down at me and tilted his head to the side, and then I could see his face again. With one eyebrow raised, he said, "Don't call me that. That's what I called my father. Call me something else."

I don't remember how the rest of the conversation went, but by the end of the walk we'd agreed that I would call him Papa.

I'm sure my father thought of his own father during the long train ride from Brooklyn to Buffalo in June of 1988. He'd made up his mind to at least be there for the birth.

"He fell in love with you right away," my mother told me, on our second bottle of wine, surrounded by their letters. She said the conversation shifted at that point from whether or not to build a life together to what exactly that life would look like. Knowing that his mind changed completely once he met me is probably why I wasn't hurt to hear that he originally wanted an abortion. It wasn't me he didn't want—it was his vague notion of fatherhood and all the baggage and doom he associated with it. He didn't want to be "a father," but he loved being my father.

When my mother was pregnant with me she dreamt about owls, and when I was born with a bald head, big eyes, and a cleft lip, I looked a lot like one. This earned me my middle name, Tylluan, Welsh for owl, and gave my father a new image for his pantheon. He made several owl sculptures out of scavenged branches the summer I was born, and most of them have chubby legs like a human baby. My role in the forest cast of our family was set: my father the deer, my mother the Daphne, and me, the baby owl.

Tink moved out of the Loft shortly after her boyfriend went to see another woman give birth to his child; that was finally enough to break them up. He kept his room at the Loft as a studio space, but my mother insisted that they also get an apartment.

"I didn't want my baby learning to crawl across a carpet of metal shavings, saw dust, and cigarette butts," she said, shaking her head at the idea. The Loft had been perfect as an artist colony, but even my father couldn't argue it was a reasonable place for a baby, so they rented a small apartment close by in Greenpoint.

She also wanted him to get rid of his half-feral tomcat Catman, afraid that he would maim me, but that was where he drew the line. An important member of the Loft crew, Catman attacked my father's leg in a bodega in Greenpoint, and he took him home in a cab when the old Polish lady who ran the place decided he was too vicious to stay in the store as a mouser. Catman had as much of a tough-guy attitude as the men he lived with, and my father was maybe the first cat owner to truly appreciate the gifts of dead birds and rodents his loyal familiar proudly presented him with. I can see the two of them now: my father crouched down, dismembering a dead bird to save its wings for sculpture material; Catman watching, purring, proudly licking the blood off of his chops. Twisted, and sweet.

Luckily, Catman channeled his toughness into protecting me, and became my guard cat. He sat stoically next to my crib while I slept, next to me on the floor while I stacked blocks. He once launched himself at my mother, claws drawn, when she was tickling me and he mistook my shrieks for genuine distress. My parents told me he was my big brother, which I believed until I went to kindergarten and realized that all of the other kids' siblings were human. It hadn't seemed out of place to me: deer-father, tree-mother, owl-baby, and cat-brother.

My parents got married at City Hall on May 19, 1989—two years after they met and just under a year after I was born. My mother wore a forest-green dress suit and I wore a floral-print dress with white lace tights. The cake said "Congratulations Lilly" on it—Mark's idea.

My mother keeps the pictures from that day in their own special album, and I took it out to look at them when I visited her in the midst of all of these long talks. I remember looking at them when I was little, too. The excited *holy shit we're really doing this* looks on both of their faces, my mother holding me while the justice of the peace says his part and they grin at each other like goofy, in-love kids. I cried during the ceremony because I wanted to nurse, and there are lots of pictures of me sulking and frowning. They both look so young, so healthy.

They took a leap, holding onto the impossible hope that a couple who'd met at a strip bar and carried on a secret affair that resulted in an accidental pregnancy after only a few months could somehow attain stable marital bliss.

Birth announcement: Woodcut on paper

Opposite page: "Tylluan:" Carved wood,
scrap metal, 15″ (Photographed at the
home of Heidi O'Donnell, Phoenicia, NY)

Carved wood, scrap metal; 15″

Top: Seed pod and wood, 3.5"
(Photographed at the home of Heidi O'Donnell, Phoenicia, NY)

Bottom: Kitchen table drawing: Pencil on paper

By my senior year at the New School, I was still bartending at night and maintaining an almost perfect GPA while spending thirty hours a week crouched over my desk in the corner of the newspaper office, debating every little decision like it was life or death. I applied to Columbia's journalism graduate program partly because it felt like the next logical step, and partly because I wanted to see if I could get in—if my hard work would translate beyond this specific tiny student publication. I told myself I'd only go if I got a significant scholarship, that just an acceptance would be all the validation I needed.

When I got the acceptance letter a few months later, with almost no scholarship, I understood for the first time how much I felt I had to prove. I'd been doing it subconsciously all through college: the drop-out who got the best grades, the erstwhile fuck-up whose color-coded planner made up for years of rootlessness. I never thought of it as compensating, I just thought of myself as someone who'd gotten her shit together. But then I got accepted to Columbia, the stamp of institutional approval I didn't realize I'd needed so badly, and I imagined the sweet vindication of becoming a high school drop-out with an ivy league master's degree.

I thought of the guidance counselor from Bard who'd told me I'd end up on the street if I didn't "straighten up and fly right" (she really used those words), and imagined mailing her a photocopy of my master's degree with "FUCK YOU, CUNT" written across it in Sharpie. I thought of my mother, so pleased and proud, so relieved I'd "turned out ok," and how she should have taken my word for it when I said I knew what I was doing, that I didn't need high school to get where I wanted to go in life. And I thought of my father, how he would have done a silly little dance, how he would have told strangers at the grocery store that his daughter was going to Columbia. He would have come and sat with me on a bench on campus, tucked away in a quiet corner that looked like the Cloisters. We would have sat on that bench together while he said over and over to himself, to me, to the squirrels chittering by, "Wow! A Schactman in the ivy league!" And then we would have explored the library together for hours, and every time I looked up I would have caught him beaming at me.

Scholarship or not, I had to go.

Journalism appealed to me as a way to have a respectable career and a more stable life than my parents ever did, but still move freely around the edges of society and challenge authority and follow my own interests wherever they led me. And I liked the idea of translating and synthesizing information into something anyone could understand; I wanted to collect stories like my father collected scraps of metal and wood, seeing the beauty in the small things that others might overlook. Or maybe I just wanted to collect a master's degree as one more gift for a dead man.

I still don't really know what stability means, or if it's a real thing that's possible to attain. But I know that when you don't have it, it seems like the promise of safety. Like redemption. But it can also feel impossible—the steps that are necessary to reach it don't come naturally if they're not what you're used to, like joining a dance class three weeks into their study of a new combination. When you don't know how to do the things you're expected to do, it can be so much easier to declare them bullshit and say you never wanted to be a part of it anyway. But how sweet to fall into step, to feel like maybe you know what you're doing just enough to fake your way to that magic place called stability, where you'll finally be able to let your guard down.

The first day of classes, I got off the subway at 116th Street almost an hour early. I didn't want to show up late and let everyone know right off the bat that I was a screw-up in disguise, and I wasn't sure how long it would take to get there—the only times I'd ever gone that far uptown were to meet my ecstasy dealer in Spanish Harlem when I was fifteen, and that was never an appointment with a specific start time. I came up the subway stairs and stared at the big stone entryway, the long tree-lined brick path that cut straight through the campus, pastoral in the middle of Manhattan, and I turned and walked in the other direction. Heading down Broadway looking for coffee, I passed a Starbucks but kept going. I needed cheap, watery, slightly burnt deli coffee with too much milk and sugar. Something familiar to take with me into that foreign place.

Walking back, I held my coffee in both hands like I was warming them on a winter day, even though it was August and balmy. I was still early, but decided I should find the journalism building anyway. The last thing I wanted was to get there early but then still be late to my first class because I got lost in the twists and turns of the campus. I exhaled as I walked through the entryway, down the brick path full of bubbly undergrads traveling in groups. I walked to the center, which opened up to the huge quad with the two giant libraries on either side and the iconic statue on the steps, and stood with my mouth slightly ajar like a tourist. I did get lost, walking back and forth on that path three times before I found Pulitzer Hall, but I still had fifteen minutes to spare.

I sat on the stone steps and drank my shitty coffee and tried to draw the surroundings into myself enough that I would become them, enough to convince myself this was the world I belonged to. I reminded myself that from the outside, nobody could tell how out of place I was. I wore a loose-fitting white linen button-down shirt that covered my tattoos and gray slacks with sensible flats. All the dye was grown out of my hair, and I'd replaced my playful pink glasses frames with nondescript tortoiseshell. I looked like just a regular nerd, and felt like I was pulling off an epic subterfuge.

Being at Columbia felt as rebellious as dropping out of high school, both going so completely against what was expected of me.

Conventional wisdom says that the most important part of graduate school is the social connections you make, and it was clear from the first day I walked into the orientation mixer at Columbia—in the big airy lecture hall with marble floors and delicately-carved wood window frames, my new classmates milling around in their tailored blazers, with their Twitter handles written on their name tags and charming smiles plastered on their faces—that everyone had had that wisdom drilled into them so hard that, ironically, it made it impossible to genuinely connect. It felt like we were all auditioning for each other at all times, putting on the best show to make the best impression just in case the kid sitting next to you became an important editor someday. It was exhausting, and it was a kind of interaction that I felt utterly unequipped for. It was a certain kind of always being "on," a carefully crafted performance that I'd missed the training for. I suspected they taught it early in wealthy families.

By the end of the first semester, I knew I'd made a mistake. I'd been seduced by prestige, enrolled just because they'd accepted me, without stopping to think about what kind of writer I wanted to be and whether this program would help me get there. According to Columbia, it seemed, journalism was a specific set of procedures that could be memorized and endlessly replicated. There was no sense that there's art to be found anywhere in the profession; the program was all logistics, no poetics. There were two classes I enjoyed: History of Journalism, because there was a focus on the big foundational ideas and what journalism is in the context of society that got me excited about how words can shape the world; and Magazine Writing, because it was the only class where we actually discussed the craft of writing. The rest felt like it might as well be trade school. I understood what my father meant by "art school kills the artist" more than I ever had before, and felt like this training was bleeding me dry of any passion I may have had for the work.

I considered cutting my losses and quitting before I was charged for the second semester's tuition, but I figured that if I was going to be $40,000 deeper in debt for nothing, I might as well be $80,000 deeper with something to show for it. Plus, I told myself: Drop out once and you're forging your own path; drop out twice and you're just a fuck-up who can't finish what she starts.

My disillusionment was solidified during the second semester when my class took a bus tour of the Bronx. It was meant to offer insight into a part of the cultural and socio-economic landscape of the city that's rarely put front and center, to open the eyes of students who thought only of Greenwich Village and Wall Street when they thought of New York City. It felt like a poverty safari. *And over there on your left you'll see the urban poor. Be careful now, keep your hands inside the vehicle at all times.* It made it crystal clear that even if I wore the right clothes and referenced the right texts to blend in with these rich kids, I would never be one of them. I didn't need a bus tour to know what dilapidated public housing looked like; I didn't need a very patient community center volunteer to explain what subsidies low-income New Yorkers rely on. As he explained WIC, the women, infants, and children food program, I remembered taking Jael's WIC card to the grocery store when Riley was a baby, and how there were strict limits on what you could use it to buy: milk, cereal, bread. Everything else we still had to pay for with our pooled waitressing tips, which we counted and recounted to make sure we could cover everything. I remembered my own mother walking ten blocks out of her way with heavy bags of groceries, embarrassed to use food stamps at the store closest to our apartment, and crying at the counter in one bureaucratic office after another, clutching stacks of paperwork, begging for help, while I sat wide-eyed next to her.

In a local reporting class, someone whose assigned beat was Williamsburg pitched a story about how all the artists were being forced out of the neighborhood by gentrification. I couldn't take it anymore and blurted out, "Sorry but you're at least fifteen years late to that story." I hadn't meant it to come out so harsh, but pitching a story about the gentrification of Williamsburg years after Williamsburg had become synonymous with hipsters and with the very idea of gentrification itself was just too perfect an encapsulation of how out of touch the whole program felt. Like we were going through the motions of journalism but not connected to the real world in any way—not connecting with people or uncovering anything new or exciting, or literally any of the things I was there to do. I didn't look up to see the surprised faces of my classmates, but the teacher thanked me for the local perspective and asked if I could elaborate. I regretted saying anything.

By the time I walked across the stage and collected the $80,000 piece of paper I'd hoped would knock the poor-kid chip off of my shoulder, impress my dead father, and prove I was stable and "ok," I was completely uninterested in the news business—and in social climbing and class jumping and blending in and proving anything to anyone.

The jobs people were excited about right out of school were hyper-local news—city councils and street fairs and zoning disputes—or niche markets like writing for real estate or law trade publications. I understood, then, why someone might choose to be a starving artist.

Despite a complete lack of interest, I applied for a few of these jobs; because I was supposed to, because otherwise what was the point of all that work and debt. I was offered a job as a city reporter with DNAinfo—a good job with a decent salary and full benefits. It was everything I'd been working toward. It was more money than my mother had ever made. It was stability. But everything in my body recoiled from it. I felt like I had before I dropped out of high school, like I couldn't possibly force myself to do this. I didn't want to take the job and let them waste time training me only to quit after a few months, so I declined as politely as I could.

I realized that I didn't want a writing job; I just wanted to write. And I felt like an asshole when I realized that the story I most wanted to tell was the one I'd been investigating and reporting since before Columbia, the one I'd shelved for a year to focus on grad school. The one subject that really made me want to work like a reporter, chasing down every lead and uncovering secrets and blowing accepted truths wide open: the story of my father.

Most of the people I spoke to in my search, I spent a few hours with. Usually one long interview, sometimes a few follow-up questions over the phone or email. But with my mother I just kept digging, and kept finding new depths. We spent dozens of hours, stretched over years, talking about her relationship with my father, her perspective overlapping and interweaving with everything else I'd found. Each conversation felt like she'd finally borne her soul to me, but I always found more bubbling up later: more details, more truth, more pain, more ugliness.

My mother was sexually abused while in foster care as a young child. She repressed the memories of what happened to her for years, but as a young adult, some of those memories started to sneak back in through cracks in her subconscious armor. This was when she first started using heroin, the year before she met my father. Then when I was three years old, seeing me run around happy and innocent like she had been before she was victimized, and feeling the weight of the responsibility to keep me safe, brought it all flooding back with renewed force. Everything she'd held off for twenty years rushed in and consumed her, and it was like the trauma was fresh all over again.

She explained all of this to me, sitting in the floral armchair I'd found on the street and hauled up four flights of stairs so we didn't have to sit on the floor anymore. I sat in my desk chair, turned around to face her. Our knees were a foot apart from each other in that tiny room that was not really big enough for two chairs. Up close, huddled together, the physical opposite of what our relationship had been for so long. She pulled her feet up onto the chair and wrapped her arms around her shins. I thought *she's so tiny*, and then remembered that we have the exact same frame.

We'd skipped right over this period in our first several interviews, but finally it came out as we circled back again and again.

She took a deep breath and told me about how she finally decided she needed to start seeing a therapist. She was coming apart, and needed help. My father tried his best to be supportive, but he felt threatened. His tight-lipped Midwestern upbringing hadn't prepared him to think of therapy as a positive thing. Barry would never have approved. She told me he was afraid that if she went, she'd discover that he was a fraud, not really up to the job of husband and father.

"He wanted to know everything that happened every time I went," she said. "He would pick me up after and instantly start asking questions about what we talked about. He had no idea how ridiculous that was. It didn't take long before he decided that my therapist hated him."

He told her they would get through this rocky period together, not to feel bad for being a mess, that he'd be patient. But even while saying all the right things, he pressured her to have sex. In the midst of her dealing with serious sexual trauma, he was unable to put his own desires aside long enough to give her the space she needed to process her abuse.

I'd never questioned, or even thought too directly, about the idea of my mother as Daphne. It was just something she was. My mother, the beautiful, alluring, mythical tree-woman. Natural and wild, growing at the edge of the water, roots in the ground and leaves draped protectively, or maybe provocatively, like the bangs that sometimes fell over her eyes.

My father putting her in the pantheon of his symbols as a woman in the trees—finding her body as he carved into branches—seemed like devotion. Like awe. But as my mother told me this part of the story, I remembered that Daphne was trying to escape. Her transformation into a tree wasn't the communion of woman and nature; it was a last resort when she couldn't get away from the man who was chasing her. It was her retreating into herself and leaving herself behind, disappearing, hardening into a tough bark.

So fluent in symbols, my father must have been aware that Daphne's story is not exultant, it's tragic. If my mother was Daphne in the story of their love, what did that make him? The pursuer, the relentless, from whom she had to withdraw. He feigned like he didn't know what he was doing to her with his persistence, but still he created her as a woman destroyed by it.

He wouldn't leave her alone, wouldn't stop begging and cajoling and manipulating her for sex, she said, waiting for her in her own bed, where she was supposed to be safe.

"I didn't know I had the right to say no," she said, her voice wavering with sadness for the girl she'd been and discomfort at the idea of casting my father as the villain in this story. "The only way I knew how was to get him out of the house."

So she told him to go, and he moved back into the Loft. This period is why I have early childhood memories of the Loft—I went back and forth between the apartment we'd all lived in, upstairs from a butcher shop on Lorimer Street, and the Loft. I got to slip into the life my father had had before he was a family man, to be part of his artist colony and hang my paintings on the walls with the rest. I didn't know, of course, why he was living there. At three years old, I was too young to even really understand that my parents weren't living together. The Loft was just a fun place I went sometimes, sleeping huddled under an electric blanket with Papa and Catman on cold winter nights in the drafty, unheated factory building.

"I missed him right away," my mother told me with a sad little shrug. She knew she needed to get him out of the house to protect herself, but she didn't fully understand how egregious his behavior had been, would never have thought at the time to call it abusive—a word that hung unspoken but clear in the air around us as she told this part of the story. And she missed the little family they'd made together. So after a few months, she let him move back in.

When they were back together, he started drawing and sculpting rabbits, showering her in them, hanging them in the kitchen, covering the shelves in the bedroom with them. My mother is hesitant to analyze his work, or to attach any simplified meaning to the symbols, but, "The rabbits were about being mine," she said, without any doubt. "I know that." It was understood between them that he was the rabbit, and that the "X" the rabbits were often depicted with meant love.

"A lot of the rabbits were bound in one way or another—that speaks for itself, at least on the surface," she said. She treasures the rabbit pieces now that he's gone—she has one hanging next to her bed, another on her dresser, another on her bookshelf, tangible reminders of how loved she was. But at the time he was making the rabbits, she resented them.

"It was like I was pushing him away but he always had this way of expressing how much he was mine and how much he needed me and needed me to need him," she said. "It was like he kept telling me how he felt without talking when I wouldn't let him keep talking or keep throwing himself at me when I didn't want him."

He was calling out to her with rabbits like he had called out to Cathy with dogs—surrounding her with physical depictions of his love for her. There's something romantic about such a grand gesture, but also suffocating: Even when he promised to give her space, he filled that space with symbols of his devotion. He even got one of his rabbit drawings tattooed on his back.

I'd assumed she would be eager to tell her side of the story, but once we got into it I saw that this wasn't easy for her. She always says she doesn't have a good memory, but then she called up all of these details and it was like she could swing herself directly back into everything she'd felt then. For the first time, I saw her emotional fluidity as an elegance and a skill, not always a trap to be avoided. I realized, too, what a gift she was giving me, baring all of this old pain just because I asked her to.

I knew that my father adored my mother, thought she was unbelievably beautiful and constantly stopped to admire her. But I never realized there was such an ugly side to this admiration, that it was a sometimes violent, possessive love. I strained to visualize that dark side, and I waited. I waited for something in me to shatter, for my memory of him to shift—I waited for my idealized, mythologized vision of my father to distort now that I knew about this selfish, coercive side of him. I felt like it should. But it didn't.

I waited some more, lying on my couch with the lights dim, fighting off any denial defense mechanisms, replaying my mother's shaking voice in my head. And I found that somehow I could hold these two images in my mind at once: the brutish, demanding husband who compounded his young wife's sexual trauma; and my father, endless source of art supplies and projects, who used to wink at me with conspiratorial glee after making references to inside jokes, even when we were alone. The two versions of him existed together in my mind, butting up against each other, contradicting each other, but neither erased the other. I could see more, could see deeper into the story, but the parts I remembered and cherished remained unchanged. Like the frame of the image expanded to show more around the edges, but what had always been at the center stayed the same.

The more I thought about it though, the more I wondered if it was less that this new part of the story didn't alter what I knew of my father and more that I simply couldn't reconcile the two. Something in my mind protected my memory of my father by walling it off from this idea of him as an antagonist; created a whole other version of him, like a separate character, distinct from the father I loved.

"Rabbit Contemplating X:" Woodcut on paper

I needed some way to test my memory, something physical and tangible I could measure it against to help me understand what was real—or how real anything could be if it was such a small part of the story, missing so much context. So on a cool autumn morning, I took the L train out to Bushwick and made a pilgrimage to the old Loft.

In the first block after the train station, there was only one business that didn't fit with my memories—real or handed down—of the neighborhood, a hip-looking restaurant called Harefield Road. There was an art supply store called Artist & Craftsman Supply—the sign out front said it was established in 1985, two years after the guys moved into the Loft, and I wondered if they believed it had opened especially for them.

There was only one shiny, new apartment building on the walk so far, and it rose a modest two stories above the squat brick buildings on either side—it didn't loom over them, drooling glass and steel down their necks like the ones in the East Village. This was 894 Metropolitan; I was getting close to 1000, to the Loft.

Though I only lived at the Loft briefly, part-time, and when I was very young, a disproportionately large amount of my early childhood memories take place there. They're just snippets: riding my Fisher Price car in circles around the cavernous living room and seemingly endless labyrinths of hallways and makeshift bedrooms, burrowing into scratchy wool blankets and eating grilled chicken during rooftop barbeques at night while Mark sang Johnny Cash songs and let me believe he'd written them for me. Me and my cousin Sabina, a year younger than me, playing "circus," a game that consisted of covering each other's faces with stickers. Me in Papa's bedroom, which in my memory looks as big as a darkened concert hall, dictating stories about the creation of the universe while he dutifully took them down in little hand-bound books of brown paper. Him reading Grimms' fairy tales to me while I painted illustrations for them.

The kitchen was the only room with any heat, so the guys would spend all winter sitting around the long, splinter-covered table, talking about what they were working on, giving criticism, praise, and suggestions, and making jokes I didn't understand, laughing loudly with teeth full of coffee grounds.

As I got closer, I noticed that the sidewalks looked like they hadn't been repaired or replaced since the day when I was three years old that my father told me he liked cracked sidewalk squares because they reminded him of spider webs. The air retained the industrial smell of paint and fumes from the auto-repair shop that still stood on its own little triangular block, formed by the intersection of two diagonal streets. Breathing in that bouquet mixed with the smell of rain-wet concrete, I could have closed my eyes and been back in 1991.

With so much connected to it, I assumed I'd recognize the building when I saw it. I passed 980 and knew I was almost there. I looked ahead a bit and saw...a U-Haul rental lot. I stopped walking, stopped breathing. I was prepared to come back and see my childhood block completely changed; even ready for the Loft to have been converted into a store or a restaurant, or worse, expensive renovated apartments. But I was not ready for the building to be gone entirely. If it had been converted there would still be traces of the old Loft to seek out, but if it was gone I would never know if it was really real. Memories are so intangible and slippery, I just wanted there to be one solid place, a building I could lay my palm against, that would draw them down to earth.

Then I noticed the unmarked, windowless metal door of the building just past the U-Haul lot, with two crumbling concrete steps leading up to it, and I exhaled. This was it.

There was no light inside and some of the windows were covered in cardboard. I looked up and down the street and, seeing nobody coming for blocks in either direction, I set my tote bag down on the sidewalk and took a running jump at the side of the building, grabbing onto the bars on one of the windows with both hands. Walking my feet up the crumbling brick wall, I pulled my face up to the window. I couldn't see far inside—it was so dark. But there was a pile of construction material and miscellaneous junk that looked like it could have been there for years. It looked like the building was empty again, and I had a brief fantasy of prying open the bars on the windows and moving back in. From what I could see, it hadn't been gutted. For all I knew, the penny I glued to the kitchen floor twenty years ago was still there.

I let go of the bars and jumped down, wiping my hands on my jeans and examining the deep red impressions the bars had made on my palms. I picked up my bag and crossed the street to appraise the building from afar.

Sitting cross-legged on the sidewalk on the other side of Metropolitan, I couldn't believe how small the Loft building was. Remembering how exhilaratingly high up I felt when we barbecued on the roof, I skeptically measured the two stories through a squint. The fact that the building took up most of the block only added to the appearance of it slouching.

I pictured the Loft ceilings fading into imperceptible heights, and I just couldn't imagine them fitting into this unassuming little pile of bricks. Even the fact that I was a physically tiny child couldn't account for the discrepancy. It must be the same magic as all of Narnia fitting into a wardrobe.

I'd set out to find some clear measure of how my memory fit into reality and vice versa, but I'd only found more evidence that they could both exist even if one seemed to disprove the other. I didn't know what I would find next that would contradict what I thought I knew, but I was afraid to find out, even after years of this search. I'd reached a turning point, the part of my father's story that intersected with my own memories, with the stories I told myself about my life and who I am at the most essential level. What if I found the real story, and the life I remembered couldn't possibly have fit inside?

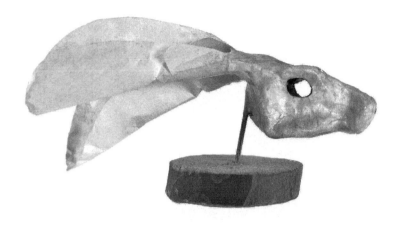

Top: Papier-mâché; 7.5" (width)

Bottom: Plaster and wood; approx. 10" (width)
(Photographed at the home of Heidi O'Donnell, Phoenicia, NY)

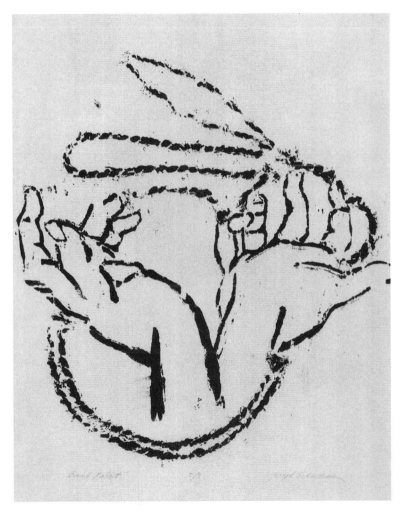

"Bound Rabbit:" Rope print and ink drawing on paper

Top: Carved wood, human hair; approx. 6″ (width)
(Photographed at the home of Heidi O'Donnell, Phoenicia, NY)

Bottom: Carved wood, rope; approx. 9″
(Photographed at the home of Heidi O'Donnell, Phoenicia, NY)

Carved wood, rope 19.5″
(Photographed at the home of
Heidi O'Donnell, Phoenicia, NY)

"I want you to know, I never did drugs when I was pregnant with you," my mother told me over the phone.

We'd talked about my parents' relationship—that cinematic night they met, the romantic escape to the woods that brought them me, his doubts about fatherhood and how I won him over, the hard time when he left and came back. We'd gone over and over all of it. But eventually, we had to get to the drugs. We'd finally had a long conversation about what she knew about my father's drug use, when it overlapped with hers, periods of time when they were both doing better. And she called me a couple of days after that conversation to make sure I had this one point clear.

"I stopped as soon as I found out," she said, for emphasis, then added: "We both did."

She insisted that they both stayed clean for the first few years of my life. I believed her and I didn't believe her. I believed that she stayed clean. And I believed that she believed him when he told her that he was clean, too. But I wasn't sure if I believed that he really was. As much as I wanted to think that we had a few wholesome years together, the animal family, it sounded too good to be true. It sounded like a lie an addict would tell his wife.

I listened as my mother described again how lovely those first few years were; how in love they were with each other, with me. "It was a really happy and sweet time," she said, more than once. She painted such a sunny picture, the nostalgia thick in her voice. My mother was living alone in the mountains upstate without much human contact, and in poor health. I hesitated to taint her sweet memories of happier times. But I couldn't help it.

"He might not have told you if he was using then," I said finally. More coldly than I meant to.

Silence on the other end. A deep sigh. And then, very quietly, all of the reminiscing fondness gone, "You're right. I really don't know how much he lied to me."

The picture does start to become clearer, though, when my parents started using together again in 1992, when I was four. My father moved back in with us after his brief return to the Loft. He showered my mother with rabbit drawings to profess his devotion. Then she went back to stripping for the first time since I was born, and found herself surrounded by cocaine.

"I thought I was healthy enough to just go make money," she explained, meaning she thought she could go dance her shift and leave without getting drawn back into the culture of the strip bars, which was a culture full of drugs—especially now that she was working at the Baby Doll Lounge, which was notoriously sleazy, in addition to Billy's, which was just regular sleazy.

It wasn't long before she started calling Joe from the payphone inside the bar during her shifts, asking if she should "bring anything home." I pictured the scene: My mother, 26 years old and beautiful, cheekbones like razor blades. A faded t-shirt thrown over her patent-leather stripper costume, curling the silver phone cord around her twitchy fingers, looking out through the window of the rickety phone-booth door at the spotlights of the stage. Calling home, sometimes to ask how her child was doing, sometimes to decide how high they were going to get later.

At first, she said, it was a weekend thing. They'd get a babysitter and go out to the Nightingale, a bar on Second Avenue owned by Tom

Hosier from the old New Haven crew, where we also sometimes went together as a family. I drank Shirley Temples and befriended the old drunk named Willy who was always slumped over on the same stool at the end of the bar and always pointed out that our names rhymed. I felt comfortable on a bar stool at four years old, something I joked about later when I started bartending; the fact that my Shirley Temples always came with at least ten Maraschino cherries was my first taste of what it's like to get special treatment as a friend of the bartender. I regaled the other Nightingale regulars with intricate stories about my dolls, Greek myths, facts I'd learned about owls. They nodded along intently, just like they did when the grown-up drunks rambled on about their idiosyncratic fascinations.

When my parents first started using together again they'd go out to the Nightingale with a big bag of coke and stay up all night. "Then it became all weekend," my mother said.

Soon all pretense of casual partying was dropped and heroin reentered the equation, quickly becoming central to their lives. Any semblance of the wariness my father took from his experience with Cathy, and my mother took from her desire to protect me, disappeared and was replaced with the rationalization of addiction.

I had no idea what was going on, of course. At that age, whatever is happening around you is your normal. I liked going to the bar to see "my friends," being out of the house after dark was like a tantalizing secret. I refused to let anyone brush my hair, so it sprang out of my head in a bright blonde explosion of curls and tufts. I ran around people's feet, wearing princess dresses and little miniature versions of my father's Timberland work boots—a wild child in a wild family in a wild city.

I remember crying when my mom would leave for work at night, but she would crouch down and give me a big kiss and tell me she loved me and couldn't wait to come back home, and then my father would come and lie in my bed, his boots hanging over the edge, and read to me from our beloved tome of Grimms' fairy tales, my head on his chest as I tried to follow along on the page. After each story he read, he'd put a small pen mark next to the title in the table of contents so we could keep track. I still have the book—taped together after years of wear—and some favorites are marked a dozen times. I'd wake up early with him and he'd pour me a bowl of cereal and we'd sit at the kitchen table together while he drank his coffee before going to his construction job, and then I'd crawl into bed with my mother, who had come home quietly an hour or two earlier, and watch cartoons until she woke up. So much of that time was wholesome.

His friend Chris remembers that once, around this time, Joe called him, "sounding really grim," and said that they were having trouble making the rent. At the time, Chris was making good money doing art direction for MTV, so he wrote a check for $600 directly to our landlord in Greenpoint. He told me when I interviewed him that he was happy to help, and that it didn't occur to him until years later that the reason they couldn't make the rent was because they were spending all their money on drugs. I wasn't the only one who didn't pick up on what was happening.

In the early '90s, a wave of gentrification brought with it a new art market—the SoHo nouveau-riche needed pretty paintings for the walls of their newly renovated lofts, not the raw, sometimes ugly art he was making. Gallery owners told Joe as much, but rather than find a way to make his vision work with their demand, he told them to go fuck themselves and went back to his studio to sulk.

"At the time it seemed noble, but in retrospect it was not that smart," Ken said. "He was angry that the SoHo galleries didn't want to show his work, but ultimately I don't understand how he could expect them to when he was so antagonistic toward them."

He refused to tailor his work to what gallery owners were interested in, insisting that they were "chicken-shit morons" and "fucking idiots" when they suggested that his work—often very large and sometimes disturbing to look at, might not be mantelpiece material. He made a six-foot-tall wooden sculpture of a naked woman with her feet wide apart, bending down to touch the ground, her vulva at eye level. The whole piece was painted pink. The Pink Lady, as she was called, was a great, attention-grabbing gallery piece, but he can't have expected anyone to put her in their living room. Even Alan from Civilian Warfare admitted that as much as he personally loved the dog masks, they were "a hard sell."

I can't imagine living without my father's work all over my walls. But now that I think about it, I can see how someone who's not used to it might not want a giant alien woman's crotch staring at them while they eat dinner, or a sculpture made out of literal roadkill hanging above their couch.

I never knew he was so insecure, that he had so much to prove to himself, to his peers, to the art world. As much as he wanted to make "art for its own sake" without considering what the galleries wanted, he still let them influence his work by straining so hard to avoid their influence. If he had played the game a little, had the confidence to believe that nobody who ever met him or saw his work doubted his artistic integrity for a second, he might have been a happier man and more commercially successful artist.

I've tried to learn from his self-sabotage, to balance the idea of writing that exists only for itself with the need to play by at least some of the rules if I want to build a career. But when agents and publishers and well-meaning colleagues suggested to me over and over again that I could sell a memoir about my father so much more easily if I took out all of the art images, I heard his voice in my head, scoffing, "fucking idiots."

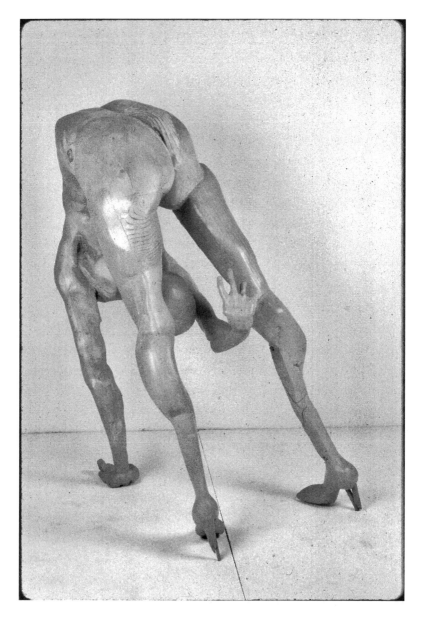

"The Pink Lady:" Carved and painted wood, approx. 72"
(Scan from the original artist slides. The Pink Lady deteriorated
beyond repair and was left in the woods in the Catskills)

When I finished grad school and realized I didn't want any of the jobs it had trained me for, my old bosses from Sophie's were getting ready to open a new bar on Sixth Street. The owner, Richie, asked if I could handle night shifts on my own—I'd previously only worked busy nights when there were two bartenders on. "Sometimes we get some weirdos, you know," he said.

"I grew up in this neighborhood, remember?" I told him. "I may be small but I can handle weirdos." I put up my fists like I was ready to box him. He laughed and gave me three nights a week, and I gratefully became part of the opening crew of Josie's, my second home for the next five years.

After trying to fit myself into the ivy league world like too-tight shoes, it was such a relief to put on cut-off jean shorts and a cropped Siouxsie and the Banshees t-shirt and stay up all night with locals, drinking whiskey and playing pool and blasting the Buzzcocks on the jukebox. I bleached my hair Courtney Love blonde and wore red lipstick every night. I stopped holding in all the bitchy comments that came into my mind—when you're behind a bar, bitchiness comes off as sass, and customers love it—and I felt free.

All the brassy loud toughness I'd cultivated as a teenager and then tried to shove down in college and grad school found a productive outlet in breaking up fights and projecting my voice to yell "No drinks on the pool table!" and "One at a time in the bathroom!" twenty times a night, loud enough to be heard over the music and the din. At first I felt guilty rejecting fake IDs considering how often I'd used one myself just a few years earlier, but I quickly developed a protective love for the bar, and took pride in maintaining order there. And my old alcohol tolerance found a use, too, allowing me to do shots with customers all night long so they all felt special, and still be able to settle out the register properly at the end of the night.

I'd been trying for so long to strive for something else, something beyond what was familiar to me. I'd tried to convince myself that I wanted to be a yuppie, that if only I could summer in the Hamptons and afford a matching living-room set, everything would be ok. But letting the strain of that reach go slack was the relief of coming home. Here, I finally felt like a more adult version of myself, not like I was wearing a costume of what I thought an adult should look like.

The bar kept me connected to the neighborhood, which kept me connected to myself. Shooting the shit with neighborhood guys brought New York City back into the cadence of my speech, after two private schools had almost wrung it out. There was Buddy, the mostly-blind electrician with the old-school New York accent where toilet is "ter-lit" and radiator is "rah-diata"—I knew him from my time working at Sidewalk because he did all their handiwork, and he had installed a stained-glass light fixture I found on the street for me. He drank Jack and Coke with no ice (he didn't believe in drinking water, even in frozen form), and I made sure to always have one ready for him by the time he sat down. Then there were John, Roman, and Kian, the three greying gentlemen who sat at the corner of the bar and kept to themselves, and as long as I continually refilled their drinks (cider, mug of Molson, and Guinness, respectively) before they were fully empty, they'd each leave a hefty tip. They were also great for an escape conversation—if an obnoxious customer was talking my ear off, I'd go attend to the guys and get into some deep important conversation with them until the bore gave up and walked away. And George, whose gigantic English bulldog named Pincus would jump up with his front paws on the bar, waiting for a pat on the head and a treat. Then there was the younger cohort, a big crew of artist skater boys who were a little obnoxious but also sweet, and them being there brought in the young hot girls, who brought in more guys, so it worked in my favor to be nice to them and give them their first round of Buds on the house.

At first, the old-man regulars all wanted to tell me about how the neighborhood had changed, giving me the lay of the land because they assumed I'd moved here for college, like most of the people my age living in the East Village. They wanted me to know I was on their turf, that this place had history and rules of its own. If they were talking about the '80s I'd say, "So my mother tells me;" if they were talking about the '90s I'd say, "I was a little kid, but I remember;" and if they were talking about some general, non-specific "old days," I'd say, "Yeah, I remember the first time we saw college frat bros unloading a U-Haul on Ludlow Street, it was all downhill from there," and then they'd understand that I wasn't an interloper and they'd stop posturing. Sometimes, if I was already annoyed and didn't feel like proving myself to anyone, I'd just say, "Yeah, sure is a shame I can walk home alone after my shift at five in the morning these days without getting mugged and raped!" with a big smile, and that would shut them up, too.

Working three nights a week left me plenty of time to write. I freelanced a little, writing about the closure of the iconic East Village shithole Mars Bar for *New York* magazine, glad it was me who got to write an ode to that place, someone who'd actually hung out there rather than some transplant dispatched to document the dying breaths of a neighborhood they'd helped destroy. I wrote about how the construction on Houston Street was crippling the beloved little hole in the wall Punjabi, which relied on the business of cab drivers who now had nowhere to park. And a profile of the Chinese lady who walked around to all the bars in the neighborhood late at night, selling cigarettes and bootleg porn DVDs. I wrote the stories about my neighborhood that I didn't trust anyone else to write. But mostly, I wrote about my father.

With Joe's connection to the art scene in New York dried up, there was nothing keeping my parents in the city. So they decided to move to San Francisco to get away from their drug-filled routine and try to start over. My mother's mother and three of her four siblings lived there, so they had a support system—and it was enough of a "real city," with an art scene of its own, to ease the blow of leaving New York for my father.

Mark suggested when we spoke again later that another reason they decided to move was because Joe owed money to everyone he knew, and didn't have any friends left because of it. Even their relationship was strained after years of being a pair—Mark said he just couldn't be around his old friend when he was so strung out, and he didn't want to be asked for money anymore.

"It's called a geographical cure," my mother said, snickering a little at their naïve hope that moving across the country would cure their addictions and solve their relationship problems—especially to San Francisco, a city famous for its drug culture. But when I was five years old, right before I started kindergarten, that's exactly what we did.

I'd been to San Francisco to visit my mom's family there once before and was excited when my parents told me we were going back. They didn't tell me, however, that we were going for good this time—

an omission I held against them for years as I demanded to go home, insisted that the only thing I wanted for dinner was pierogis from Christine's, and cried during our first winter in California because the lack of snow made me afraid that something was seriously wrong.

When we first arrived, we stayed with my grandmother Stephanie and my uncle Jake, who's four months older than me. That was the first of three times in our lives that Jake and I would live together, and the start of a close uncle/niece relationship that's our version of brother/sister. I was used to being the lone kid among grown-ups— the little girl at the bar or the gallery opening. And while Jake had four siblings, the one closest to his age, Deva, was fourteen years older than us—and the three girls were all grown up with kids of their own, my mother the oldest. Suddenly Jake and I both had a constant playmate our own age, and we were thrilled. I wasn't paying attention to my parents' strained efforts to get clean and make a life for us in a new city; my memories of that time are mostly of playing "Power Rangers" with Jake, a game where we stacked all the pillows and blankets in the house into a "monster" on his futon bed and then toppled them with flying kicks and our child-approximations of "karate sounds."

Eventually we moved into a series of apartments, and finally an actual house with a backyard and a basketball hoop over the separate garage that became my father's studio. He taught me to dribble the ball, and took turns shooting with me for hours, in his jeans and work boots.

My parents managed to stay clean in San Francisco for about a year, but then "We ran across heroin," my mother told me over the phone. "After that it was over." I could hear her shrugging, could see the face she was making, looking down and to the side like she was avoiding my eyes, even though she was home alone. Someone offered it to them once, and then they knew how to get it. It was like they had managed to convince themselves that they'd left heroin behind in New

York, literally, but once they knew it was there in San Francisco, they couldn't stay away.

Once my parents found heroin in California, or it found them, their addictions went right back to being as bad as they had been in New York, and then they got worse. Their dreams of a sunny future on the Golden Coast were quickly scrapped and replaced with plans for finding drugs and doing drugs—and constant fighting about how and when to quit.

"It's hard to live in a way that embraces the future when you're stuck like that," my mother said. "It became more about immediate problems and immediate needs."

They tried over and over again to quit, but it was that much harder, as if quitting heroin was ever easy, when one or the other would slip and inevitably drag the other down, too.

My mother said that during the weeks he was doing better he was indignant, condescending, arrogant toward her for the weakness she showed by using. But then he would slip and find himself right back at the bottom with her. When my mother tried to pull herself up, he would accuse her of the same cruelty he'd shown the week before. One always felt that the other was either judging them for using or keeping them from staying clean—holding onto each other while tumbling down a flight of stairs, each blaming the other for the fall.

Their resentment grew until they were fighting not just about heroin or money, but about fighting itself, snapping at each other constantly about the smallest things—a dish left in the sink, a piece of sculpture material accidentally mistaken for trash. They became pettier and pettier until eventually they couldn't be in the same room without screaming at each other. It was like the time we brought a new cat home and Catman didn't want her there—they circled each other around the apartment for days, staying close to the walls, fur puffed up, backs arched, trading hisses and low angry meows that sounded like faraway sirens. When my parents' hisses and barbs escalated to screaming, I would go into my room and close the door, pulling the covers up over my head and pretending I was somewhere else.

I've always remembered one fight of theirs as particularly bad, because she threw my brand-new Thermos at him and it shattered against the kitchen wall next to his head. She'd bought me that Thermos so she could pack me healthy lunches to take to school, and I knew it was expensive because she'd told me I had to eat the food she packed to make it worth the cost. I cried, recoiling from her violence.

I was being taught in first grade to settle my differences calmly and without pushing or yelling, and to consider how my actions affected others. I wondered how my parents could have missed such important lessons. I scolded them for yelling at each other, which didn't work, so I cried out of frustration, and made sure they saw me cry. The guilt didn't work either, because one of them just blamed the other for upsetting me.

Along with the stack of letters from when she was pregnant, my mother also handed over a big pile of notes written back and forth between them during this time. Most of them are from him, written early in the morning before he left for work and left on the kitchen table for her to find when she woke up. These are more painful for me to read than the pregnancy letters, because I remember this time. I remember them screaming at each other, and wishing they would remember that they loved each other. I remember hoping that my six-year-old will could hold our family together. I just didn't know what they were really fighting about. In one of these notes, he wrote:

> The basket with all of my eggs in it is: if I can get over the initial 'big sick,' put 7 clean days together, I can come back + be prepared to step back into the winged sandals of a hero. Trying and failing over + over, in full

view, is too destructive […] I don't need you, or Lilly,
to see me like this. Every step I take is on a tightrope,
+ if I take a step and don't fall off it's meaningless […]
every step that wasn't a failure, could have been.

I was so unaware of this precariousness. To me, he was steady,
strong, calm, wise, silly, loving. Everything a father should be—at
least, when they weren't fighting. But behind the curtain he was afraid,
walking a tightrope he didn't believe in his ability to walk, always living
either in failure or under the threat of it. He hid his uncertainty so well
from me.

In another letter, he wrote:

I have a house.

It's not a shithole, or a studio w/ a bed, it's a <u>house</u>.

I have a daughter,

Who I love so much that I'm frightened, I feel like the
more she becomes a full person, the more apparent
my shortcomings will become; the more visible how
unable I am to provide for her, will become.

I have a wife.

Wife is a word + I never imagined it. It's not
accurate, because it's you, <u>Heidi</u>. <u>Heidi</u>. I couldn't
want anyone else.

My father had a good, stable job at a company that made installations for natural history museums, and my mother was stripping at the

famous woman-run co-op strip bar the Lusty Lady on Market Street. There was enough money coming in, but there was never enough left. I remember hearing them in the kitchen yelling at each other over small expenditures, like name-brand cheese instead of store-brand, while I played in the living room, turning wads of cat hair into tiny nests for my Thumbelina doll to stumble upon filled with magic phoenix eggs that I'd made out of scraps of clay from my father's studio.

At the time, I just thought we were poor. I didn't know then how important money is to an addict, or how difficult to hold onto. I wasn't ashamed of being poor, or sad about it; it was just the way it was—I knew that both of my parents worked hard and assumed they were doing their best. It feels different now, knowing that they actually could have afforded to keep me in ballet classes consistently rather than letting me go back for a few classes once in a while and then pulling me out again because money was too tight, that maybe we could have gone on vacation together as a family, just one time. They allowed this thing to drain so much goodness out of our lives. I'd never thought of it that way before, but once I did, I felt cheated by both of them.

My mother explained that part of the reason they fought over money was that every two weeks, when his paycheck came in, she immediately took enough of it to make sure that I had food to eat and clean clothes to wear, and maybe even a couple of new toys. My father's idea of what was enough to survive on was distorted by his starving artist mentality. He didn't understand why I had to get new tights when the old ones ripped, or why they needed to buy me animal crackers and fruit leather when rice and beans were so cheap. He thought I should live like he always had, but my mother insisted. "I controlled the money," she told me. "If he got mad at me for it, I didn't fucking care."

I brought up the fight where she threw the thermos, and, after sighing that of course I remembered a fight that made her look bad, she explained that it started over $25 he'd spent on a used bike without clearing it with her first. She was mad because they couldn't afford it, and mad because the reason he wanted the bike was because it made it easier to get to and from their dealer.

As we paced over this time period together, my mother insisted that having enough to provide for me was a priority, even when what was left wasn't enough to cover rent, bills, and two heroin habits. Like she insisted that she didn't use when she was pregnant. Bright lines that she saw as separating a responsible drug addict mother from an irresponsible one, lines that it was important for me to see that she didn't cross. Rationalization as absolution, like if she could point out every boundary she set, she could prove she was a good mother and I came out unharmed. Addict logic.

I learned later that this was a rationalization my father shared— that he once told his friend Judith that they never let drugs affect their parenting, like they had it all figured out. They managed to get me to school most days and keep me fed, and I never found them overdosed or got taken away by Child Protective Services. So that meant, they figured, that their drug use was completely separate from the childhood I was having alongside it. Judith told me she remembered coming over to our house, seeing all of the shades drawn, the house dark and stifling, and thinking they were deluding themselves.

As a child, when I knew about it at all, I thought of addiction as this big bad demon my parents were fighting to escape from so that we could all live happily ever after. Something entirely out of their control, and not at all their fault. As I got older and heard these stories from my mother, and spent some time thinking seriously about the fact that heroin was slithering around in the background of my happiest childhood memories, I began to wonder how they could possibly bring themselves to look at the peaceful face of their sleeping child in one room, then close the door and go get high in another. It's not rational—nobody does that first bump thinking they're going to turn into an addict, and once the addiction takes over, continuing to use is the furthest thing from deliberate choice. I know all of this. But still, their drug use feels like a betrayal, and I can't help but wonder what our lives could have been like if it hadn't sucked out so much of the oxygen.

Cocaine was always around the edges when I was bartending. I could spot it immediately: a regular just a little more invested than usual in making sure I understood the point they were making, going to the bathroom more often than beer could possibly be flowing through their system. But I pretended not to notice, and on the few occasions that someone was stupid enough to offer me some, forgetting that as the bartender they should be trying to hide it from me, I said "No thanks," casually, like they'd offered me a piece of chocolate. It was mostly easy. Except for a few times when it wasn't.

There was one night when the bar wasn't actually busier than usual, but I was scrambling to keep up as one thing after another went wrong. It seemed like the keg kicked every time I tried to pour a beer, I broke a glass every time I went to clear tables, the customers all seemed drunker and rowdier and more demanding than usual. A fight broke out at the pool table, and a guy insisted that his bill was wrong because there's no way he had ordered that many shots (he had), someone puked in a bathroom sink, and every time I turned around someone had wandered outside with a drink and I had to run out and herd them back inside before a cop noticed. It felt like every sleazy old man in the neighborhood had come in that night, specifically to call me "sweetheart" and ask if I had a boyfriend, how old I was, what I liked to do for fun, until I wanted to tell them my favorite hobby was castration. The frustrations built and built all night until I felt like I might scream at the next person who asked me for anything—and there were still four more hours to go until I could close.

I went to check the bathrooms to see if there was another catastrophe I had to deal with, and spotted a full bag of coke on the floor of the women's. I locked the door behind me and stood in the still, echoing quiet of the tiny tiled room, the loud bar muffled. I just stared at it, there on the floor, my mind racing, imagining how much better my night could get. Nobody would even have to know. It had been almost ten years, but the sense memory of the chemical taste so bracing it feels cold flooded my body and I shuddered a little, with equal parts disgust and desire. I knew that if I picked that bag up off the floor and snorted it, I wouldn't stop there. I still knew Prince's phone number by heart. He was probably out of business by now, but I also remembered every single regular and fellow bartender I'd ever seen sniffle, and knew I could find a new connection in minutes if I wanted to.

I picked the bag up carefully, like it might disappear between my fingers. I held it up to the light and looked closer at the big chunks with a slightly yellow tint. My heart was racing and I didn't know how long I'd been standing in the bathroom.

Then, abruptly, before I had a chance to talk myself out of it, I dropped the bag in the toilet and flushed. Throwing it in the trash wasn't enough; I would know it was there for the rest of the night, would be mentally digging through the used paper towels. But then it was gone and the decision was made. I shook my head, washed my hands, and splashed some cold water on my face. I replaced the toilet paper roll and scooped the paper towels off the floor into the trash. I looked in the mirror and wondered what the fuck had just happened. I wondered, too, if it might have gone differently if I hadn't been so deeply immersed in my father's story, hadn't been thinking about addiction every day, and blaming my parents for being at its mercy.

I have a clear-as-a-photograph memory of looking up at the San Francisco Armory, the red bricks jutting out of the tall, imposing building, contrasting with the bright, sharp blue of the California afternoon sky. The strongest, clearest part of the memory is just that image, a flash. But I also remember, in a more watery, distant way, that while I was looking up at those red bricks and that blue sky, my mother was trying to explain inpatient rehab to me without explicitly saying what it was. By this point, at seven years old, I had started to piece together snippets of overheard conversation and understood, in the way children do, that there was some secret trouble in our lives.

"I might need to go away for a little while. To learn how to be a better mommy," she said. I kept looking up at the sky, but held her hand a little tighter in case she intended to leave right that minute. I told her she was already a good mommy.

"I could do better," she responded, gently squeezing my fingers in hers.

She didn't end up checking herself in, but I still remember that conversation as a turning point. It was her way of telling me that she was committing, for real, to getting clean—telling me what was going on without going into gory details. She couldn't bring herself to leave me for long enough to check into rehab, so she started working her outpatient program harder than ever instead.

I remember the methadone clinic. It was on a side street somewhere in the Tenderloin, facing the back of a Chinese restaurant with a vent that was always pumping out fryer smoke. She brought me with her a few times, but one trip sticks out in my mind. I was happy to go along because we'd stopped at Toys 'R' Us on the way and my mother had bought me a plastic genie doll. She was about a third the height of a Barbie and had a blonde ponytail and a pink veil over her face like Barbara Eden from Nick at Nite, and she came with a magic carpet accessory that her feet clicked into.

I swooped the magic carpet carrying the genie down the street, past the vent, and through the nondescript double glass doors into the smell of antiseptic and desperation. There were a few linoleum steps up to the waiting room, where we sat in the vinyl seats of two wooden chairs that were bolted to the floor. I was still playing with my doll, and a woman sitting across from us smiled at me. She looked tired, and her pink lipstick wasn't all inside the lines. She held her purse with both hands, clutching it so tightly that it hovered above her lap.

A nurse came out and called my mother's name, and she stood up, turning to me. "I'll be right back," she said, leaning in to point a finger in my face. "Stay right there. Don't get out of that chair. And don't talk to anyone."

As soon as she followed the nurse into a back room, I turned around and knelt on my chair so my genie could fly higher. I turned in a circle and made magical whooshing noises. When I'd spun all the way around and was facing forward again, the woman with the lipstick asked me, "What've you got there?"

"It's a genie!" I told her. I was usually shy around strangers, but I hadn't gotten a chance to show off my new toy to anyone yet and I couldn't resist.

"Wow!" she said, smiling but already not really paying attention. She started rummaging through her purse, dumping its contents onto her lap as I told her about the magic carpet. There was a pack of cigarettes, the lipstick that she was so bad at applying, and a spoon. She continued rummaging and finally pulled out the lighter she must've been looking for. I continued telling her all about how fast the carpet could fly and how my genie could get all the way to New York in five minutes, and when I got a carpet big enough I was going to go back there because that's where I was from. And then my mother came out and grabbed me by the hand, pulling me quickly outside. Yanking me behind her down the street, she said, "Don't ever talk to ladies who carry spoons in their purses."

My mother slipped sometimes, but her effort to get clean was continuous and genuine. She told me with tears in her eyes, sitting on her couch upstate, that it was her love for me that made her stop using for good. I had to admit that this was big, that even if there were so many things she had never been able to do for me, she had done this. I so often saw her as weak—too weak to handle her own emotions so that I had to help her carry them, stooped under their weight. Too weak to make life work in one place so that I spent my childhood on the run from her demons. Too weak to catch me when I was falling, hard and fast, as a teenager. But she was strong enough to quit heroin. Strong enough to do what's impossible for so many otherwise strong people. And she'd done it so that my life would be better.

But rather than sitting in that realization, rather than appreciating that my mother's love for me was strong enough to pull her through fire, all I could think was *Why didn't that work for him?* She was telling me that she loved me enough to get clean, but what I heard was that my father didn't. I know it's not that simple, but there was a part of me that was furious at him for not seeing what my mother saw—that he couldn't be a good parent and keep using. I suppose it's more accurate to say that he saw it, he must have known that, but it wasn't enough to make him stop. I was feeling what he once felt about Cathy, like the addict I loved had chosen drugs over me.

My father tried to keep up, to get clean too, but always seemed to cave—and then to beat himself up for it. Here was a clear, ugly incarnation of the Hunter/Hunted: the addict in him taking down the man. He was striving, trying so hard to escape, but the thing he was running from was inside of him.

He made a lot of art involving glass during this period; I wonder if he was thinking about fragility. Fragile marriage, fragile sobriety. Or maybe it was the sharp edges that preoccupied, their ability to wound. My mother said she stopped asking him to wash dishes because he would "accidentally on purpose" break wine glasses and then use the stems and shards as legs for Bad Barbies, which he was making a lot of in those days. He'd started making them when he was consumed with love for her, but he was a different kind of trapped now.

Whenever things would get bad enough that one or both of them was ready to give up, there would be a momentary upswing—one good meal shared together, one flower picked on the way home from work—just enough to keep them hanging on, to remind them how deeply in love they had been once, and maybe could be again.

"I know you try so damn hard + work work work," she wrote in a note that started with an apology for hurtful things said the night before. "I know that you change and bend for us more than is comfortable."

"Are we in the middle of a good groove? Are we?" He asked in another kitchen-table note, hoping for improvement but insecure in his hope, wanting her to tell him that he wasn't imagining it.

> I still notice that I'm the one who says, 'we're doing better, aren't we?'
>
> Are you rolling your eyes?
>
> Can you look me in the eyes + tell me honestly what you're feeling about us? About yourself? About me? Can you? (could you? Would you? On a boat? On a train? With a goat?)
>
> Can you tell me someday that you are happier?

Even in the midst of relative optimism he was too thrown off balance by the back and forth, too rattled by the insecurity of it.

> If 'I love you' means—I know you, I've loved you, you're Lilly's papa, then I guess my worst fears and nite-mares are just waiting to happen. + there's probably little, nothing, I can do. These are my little voices.

He was open about how terrified he was of losing her, always asking for reassurance. He was almost as afraid of losing her as he was of withdrawal, maybe even more so—right up until the symptoms started, and avoiding the big sick became the only thing he could think about.

After taking turns pulling each other down, doing the vicious dance of blame and surrender for two years, she was getting closer and closer to full recovery, and he just kept slipping further down.

He wrote:

> I've tried to be the hero, and failed. I guess nothing on this planet has the look of failure quite like that of an unsuccessful hero.

> But, I am made of hero stuff, I just need a small piece of time to get through what's buried it (what I've buried it with).

He knew he was running out of chances, that he'd have to get clean soon if there was going to be any marriage left to save.

"He had become an animal," my mother told me when I asked her to describe the lowest point. "He wasn't taking care of himself at all. He wasn't showering. He didn't care if he had clean clothes on. He was living like a pig. It became really repulsive." I winced at this, because it was the kind of thing she used to tell me about him, when it was inappropriate and cruel for her to do so. It was the kind of thing that you shouldn't tell a kid about her father—how disgusting he is, how selfish and petty and childish. But it's the kind of thing I'd asked her to tell me now. A true thing.

"I told him that if he didn't come with me to methadone it was over, and he didn't," my mother told me, with a shrug that added, *What else could I do.*

I wondered if he thought then about the ultimatums he'd given to Cathy, the pain it caused him to try to help her, to fail, and to have no choice in the end but to walk away and leave her to destroy herself. Did he see the cruel symmetry?

When he rejected the hand my mother reached back to help him, their marriage was over. I pictured them in a war zone: Him too injured to go on, her making the hard choice to save herself by leaving him behind.

She picked up more shifts at the strip club and started designing and sewing costumes to sell to the other dancers—her first clothing line, called Sew What—collecting her own money so she could afford to leave, and collecting the courage to do it.

The summer after I got back from Marin, before I started at the New School, I went camping on the old Primitive Hunting Society stomping grounds in the Catskills with Mark and Brian and the two Sabinas—my cousin Sabina, who was also Mark's goddaughter; and Brian's daughter, also named Sabina. The whole time we walked through the woods and Mark built a fire, I felt the absence of my father. He should have been there, the other half of the third pair.

After the trip, I suggested to my mother that we spread my father's ashes in the Catskills. Things hadn't been calm enough at any point since his death to have a real conversation about what to do with them, so the ashes had stayed in the box from the coroner, in my mother's closet. But now felt like the right time. I was staying with her for a while until I found a new place to live, and we were mostly getting along. We could all go up there together, I suggested—me, her, my father's sister Amy, and of course Mark and Brian would be there for a proper Primitive Hunting Society send-off.

My mother agreed it was a good idea, but when I mentioned it to Amy she said she didn't think we should invite Brian. "They didn't part on the best of terms," was all she would say, telling me I'd have to ask my mother for the whole story. I figured she was blowing whatever it was out of proportion, that whatever had happened between my father and Brian would be less important than their almost twenty years of friendship. I felt bad for both of them that they hadn't gotten a chance to reconcile before my father died, and remembered calling them "silly" for laughing together like giddy kids when they saw each other after long periods apart.

A few days after the phone conversation with Amy, I walked out into the kitchen while my mother was washing dishes. I cleared my throat and she jumped a little, turning to look at me.

"Why did Papa and Brian stop being friends?" I asked, getting straight to the point.

The look on her face told me that she'd been preparing herself for a long time for when I would ask that question, and that she'd hoped I never would. She turned the faucet off and dried her hands, wincing.

She inhaled deeply, steeling herself before explaining that she and my father had been fighting so much, that they were still living together but not "together" anymore, barely even speaking. And then right when things were at their worst between them, Brian came to visit. She explained for a long time before she finally rushed out the words, "Me and Brian slept together."

I stood in silence, leaning against the kitchen wall while she kept explaining. I could tell that she expected a reaction, so I tried my hardest not to give her one. I went cold in the eyes, flooded with anger past the point of an outburst. I felt like I owed it to my father to be furious with her. He wasn't here to hold a grudge, so I would hold it for him.

Only later, after the interviews, after my mother and I had spent hours talking about how they'd both tried so hard but in the end she couldn't stay with him and stay clean, did it start to make sense. We revisited what happened between her and Brian after we talked about the methadone clinic, about her ultimatum that my father had to go with her or she was going to leave, and about her stashing away money from the strip club, saving up to save herself. Now I understood that having sex with Brian wasn't some careless, spiteful thing she did to hurt my father, or because she didn't care. It was something she did because she didn't know how to just walk away from the love of her life, no matter how filthy and strung out he was—the only way she knew how to end their relationship was to blow it up.

I knew I had to talk to Brian. I'd been telling everyone I talked to that I wanted the whole truth, that I could handle it. *Could I?* I had to decide just how committed I was, how much discomfort I was willing to put myself through, or if maybe I could justify skipping this conversation. Of course, I knew I couldn't.

I asked Brian to meet me at Odessa, a Polish diner a few blocks away from my apartment. A quiet, neutral territory where none of the neighborhood weirdos would care what we were talking about. Brian countered that we should try a new tapas place on Avenue B instead. I hesitated, saying it might be too loud for my digital recorder to pick up our conversation, and he replied, "You want your interview subject to be comfortable, don't you?"

We were off to a bad start.

As I walked toward the restaurant, I saw him waiting outside before he saw me. The first thing I noticed was how much he looked like my father. I'd noticed this about him before, but it was especially striking in the context of this meeting. He had the deep wrinkles across his forehead, the curly gray hair pulled back into a ponytail with little poufs of frizz escaping at the temples. My father was still salt-and-pepper when he died, but he would have been gray by now. Brian was wearing a t-shirt and I could see his lean, strong arms that looked like my father's. I thought about those arms wrapping around my mother's waist and I wondered if she'd noticed the similarity too. I gagged a little, just as Brian looked up and saw me. He greeted me with a smile that accentuated the laugh lines around his eyes, just like my father's.

As we stepped inside, I noticed right away that it was the kind of restaurant that wishes it was a bar—music too loud for conversation, lighting too dim to see what you're eating. As I wedged myself into my seat at our tiny table crammed between two other tiny tables, I tried not to drag my shirt through anyone's plates—and prepared myself for four strangers to hear this awkward conversation we were about to have.

I didn't ask the question I was there to ask right away. I had other ground I wanted to cover before the uncomfortable stuff made any lighter conversation impossible. We picked at our tapas while Brian told me about the gallery days and the Primitive Hunting Society. He ran through stories quickly, clearly on edge. He knew why we were really there, and my working my way up to it seemed to frustrate him.

"Just ask me already!" he finally blurted out, putting me on the spot—the opposite of how this was supposed to go. I was out of wind-up questions anyway, so I took a deep breath and asked, "What happened between you and my mother?"

He told me pretty much the same story my mother had, about how unhappy my parents were together, what a mess my father was, and how she just couldn't work up the courage to leave.

"It was necessary," Brian said. Very certain. Steady. Not jumpy anymore, and a little too confident that he'd done nothing wrong. "It was necessary but destructive."

He explained that he'd met Heidi about a week after Joe did, and that they'd always had a "connection." He made it sound like it was just a matter of timing, that if he'd met her a week earlier, they might have been together all along. As if, in the grand scheme of things, him screwing the wife of one of his best friends wasn't such a big deal. I tried not to scowl. My mother's rationalization had made a certain kind of sense to me, but Brian's felt flimsy.

They never acted on their attraction, he said, until he visited in San Francisco, and then, "All of a sudden your mom and I were fucking our brains out." I felt like he was testing me, trying to make me uncomfortable. I had made him squirm by taking too long to get to the question, so now he was punishing me by being blasé about fucking my mother, while I sipped my margarita and nodded along, not giving him the satisfaction of looking scandalized.

"Your dad figured it out right away," Brian said. "It was a disaster. We never talked again."

Amy was right. *They didn't part on the best of terms.*

I said an awkward goodbye to Brian outside of the tapas bar and turned toward home, imagining how hurt my father must have been, how alone he must have felt. My cheeks still felt hot from the effort of staying calm while Brian justified what he and my mother had done.

I doubt my father ever would have forgiven Brian, but I wonder if he would have forgiven my mother. If he had eventually gotten clean and had the self-awareness to see how bad things were between them, how she needed to leave for her sake and mine, could he have understood this desperate measure?

When my parents finally split up for real, when I was seven, my mother took me and moved into a one-bedroom apartment on Lexington Street in the Mission. I got the bedroom and she slept in the large closet off of the living room. I didn't understand what was happening, just that we were moving, which was nothing new. When it finally dawned on me that Papa wasn't coming with us, I was furious—and I blamed my mother completely. I had no idea about Brian, but I knew that she was the one who took me away and left Papa behind.

I lived with her most of the time, and saw my father on weekends. In a letter from shortly after they broke up, he wrote:

> I want Lilly to have the chance to live + think that
> a real + lasting love between 2 people is possible.
> She has that w/ you. She has it w/ me. But, I'm
> afraid her memories of you and me together will be
> memories of anger and bitterness, + hurt. Someday,

somehow, I'll have to let her know just how deeply I
loved you. All she has to do is look in the mirror to
see that. I don't want her to think of me as hateful.
I don't ever want to fight with you in front of her.
I wish we could see each other, you + I, as little as
possible. As absolutely little as possible. +, it should
be, @ least calm. I don't want your friendship, we're
not friends, but we are coparents. I only want to
not hurt or poison Lilly's view of the world.

If there is <u>any</u> respect left @ all, can you use it to try
to help with this? By not displaying your hate, anger,
curses, violence, by not saying awful things about
me, to me, in front of her. I'll try to be @ least polite.

And they did try, I think, but it took another several years for them
to pull off even a veneer of civility. Picking me up or dropping me off
inevitably resulted in screaming matches, or, at best, cold, awkward
silence. I hated them for hating each other.

Once when he was late dropping me off at her apartment, she
started yelling, telling him he was selfish, inconsiderate. He hurled
back that she just liked to be mad at him, that he couldn't do anything
right in her eyes. I'd heard this back and forth so many times it was
like they were reciting a script, and I was sick of it. I decided to teach
them both a lesson, and slowly and quietly walked away. They were so
absorbed in screaming over each other that they didn't notice I was no
longer standing between them, my head bouncing back and forth like
I was watching tennis—which was exactly my point.

I got to the corner and turned back to look at them. She was
standing on our stoop, screaming down at him like a bird of prey
descending from the sky. He yelled back up at her, his arms in the air
like he was cursing God.

I hesitated, but decided to commit to this lesson I wanted to teach them, and turned the corner. I was not used to walking the streets of the Mission District alone. I felt a tingling fear in my scalp as I turned the corner and they disappeared from view, like a cat who escapes and then immediately cries to be brought back inside. But I was more angry than scared, so I kept walking. I made it to another corner and turned again onto busier Valencia Street; following the route my mother and I took together when we were running errands. I hadn't planned to get this far, and now with people rushing past me on both sides, I decided not to push my luck. I ducked into the bodega where we sometimes shopped, and fished a quarter out of the pocket of my jean jacket to buy a mini bag of waffle Cheetos. I was just putting the first square of chemical cheese into my mouth when my parents came running in together, breathless. They were relieved enough that they had found me and focused enough on telling me not to ever do that again that they stopped throwing verbal daggers at each other. For a few terrified moments, I had gotten them to stop fighting.

Despite their bitterness, divorce was never considered after the initial threats of smear campaigns. They talked about it briefly, in terms of who could make the other look worse in a custody battle, and once they had each shown their hand the subject was set aside. Who was doing better than whom at kicking a heroin addiction wasn't likely to matter much to Child Protective Services, and they weren't likely to see her job as a stripper as the exercise in female empowerment that she did, or his temporary situation crashing on a friend's couch as an acceptable stable environment for a kid. Foster care had been the start of my mother's nightmares, and the idea of me ending up there was enough to make her stay legally married to a man who, at this point, she hated with every furious, disgusted cell in her body.

"We attacked each other with the worst possible scenario and then couldn't do anything," she told me. "We never even talked about it again after that."

This detail, the likelihood that neither of my parents would have been deemed suitable by a judge, brings into relief just how bad it was—even if it felt normal to me at the time because I didn't know anything different. Over and over as I heard these stories I had to remind myself that the child my mother was talking about was me, that all of this had happened in my childhood, while I sat at the kitchen table filling out my vocabulary worksheets and eating green grapes. That it's probably true that, at least for a time, neither of my parents were really fit to look after me. As this all sank in, I was thinking about that feeling I had on Ludlow Street, when I was careening into danger and my mother couldn't help, that I was all alone and the only person I could trust to take care of me was me. I wasn't sure what was worse: knowing, as a teenager, that I had nobody to fall back on; or feeling like I did as a kid, only to learn later that my life was precarious and unstable even then.

Digging into my parents' story was feeling more and more like digging into my own flesh, tearing open scars I hadn't even known were there. I felt shaky as I moved through my daily routine, ripples of the rawness I'd felt as a teenager, the urge to blow up my life before it could implode on me. I was drinking more, staying at the bar until after closing even on my nights off. I was starting to feel like the idea that I could ever build myself a stable, peaceful life was I lie I'd lulled myself into believing. How could I, with where I'd started? The fact that I'd taken on a lifetime of debt to get a master's degree felt like a joke, a desperate attempt to cover up the truth.

I was more grateful than ever for my job at Josie's—being a bartender was a great cover for being aimless. Drinking too much and being rowdy and having a string of sloppy, unsatisfying one-night stands was all part of the persona.

Ccncrete and scrap metal; 7.5″

Woodcut on paper (This image was also printed on glass.
Fragments of one glass version have survived)

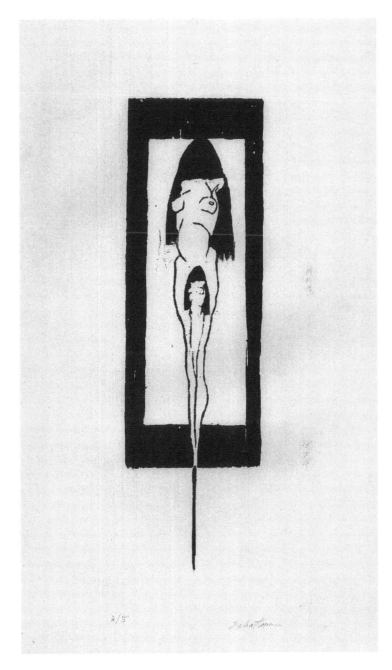

Woodcut on paper

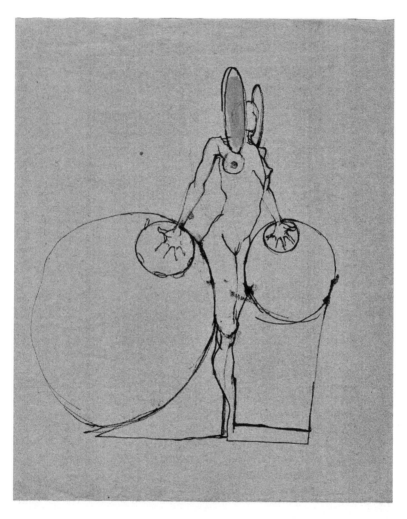

Ink drawing on paper

Early in a Sunday night shift, when I'd been working at Josie's for about a year, a guy came in who I'd seen around before. He had dramatic high cheekbones and big feathery eyebrows like Elvis, and solid, muscular arms that I kept catching myself staring at. I gave him a generic bartender "how's it goin'" and poured him a cheap beer, covertly checking my bright red lipstick in the mirror behind the register while I rang him up. While I finished setting up for my shift, moving everything behind the bar to just where I wanted it, he pulled out *Eating Animals* by Jonathan Safran Foer, leaning both elbows on the bar to read. I'd been a vegetarian since I was six, and people had been telling me to read this book about the meat industry since it came out a few years earlier.

"Oh, how is that?" I asked, remembering too late how annoying it is to be interrupted when you're reading in public, but he didn't seem to mind. He put his bookmark in and purposefully set the book down next to his beer, laying a hand on the cover, explaining that he was a cook and had been working the meat station at his restaurant for a while, so learning about this side of the industry was eye-opening. We talked about the ethics of eating meat and industrial farming and food scarcity and how much of this country's agriculture goes toward feeding livestock, and I explained that I didn't eat meat because I didn't think I could ever bring myself to kill an animal, but that I didn't try to convert anyone to vegetarianism as long as they didn't try to talk me out of it.

We talked for the rest of my shift, until I was leaning both elbows on the bar, too. His name was Soomin, and he grew up in the neighborhood. We'd seen a lot of the same punk bands play at the same venues during the same few years as teenagers, but didn't remember running into each other. We talked about how we both felt like we didn't take enough advantage of all the city had to offer because it was home, so it was always there. He said he'd been meaning to go to MoMA and I said I hadn't been in years because whenever I had a chance to go to a museum I always chose the Met. And by the time he left, we had plans to go to MoMA together. I'd been on dates with people I was already in a relationship with, but those relationships had all started with drunken hook-ups and evolved from there. I'd never been asked out like that, on a real date to get to know each other, right up front. It felt so old-fashioned and fancy and special, and I couldn't believe I had to wait a whole week until we both had an afternoon off.

It was a gray, rainy early Spring day and I was running late, speed-walking down 53rd Street. I saw him before he saw me, dressed in all black, leaning against a wall, smoking a cigarette. When he looked up and saw me watching him he smiled, and I felt my cheeks flush a little. As soon as we were inside, I couldn't help but make a snide remark at some overly-experimental painting that didn't seem to have any point other than trying to be weird, my father's judgmental artist eye deeply engrained. I wondered after I said it whether Soomin would think I was a snob, but he laughed, hard, in a way that made me immediately start thinking of what else I could say to get him to laugh like that again. After that we walked around the whole museum pointing out everything we thought was crap and laughing. At one point I noticed a few people giving us dirty looks and said, "Oops, I think we're being loud."

"Whatever," he said. "Fuck these people. If they want to come to a museum in our city they can listen to us laugh."

I remembered crying in the Met when my mother and I first moved back, and feeling exactly that way. I beamed and wanted to grab Soomin's arm and lean into him, but I didn't.

When we left, it was raining. He hailed a cab and held the door, sliding in after me. Once we were closed in the cab I could smell a faint touch of cologne on him, and while I usually hate any kind of perfume smell, I loved the idea that he'd worn it for me.

"Where are we going?" he asked me with a smile.

"Um, I don't know! We could go get a drink? Maybe at a bar where I don't work," I suggested.

We went to Blue & Gold, an old favorite of both of ours, another place we might have been at the same time without knowing it, or might have just missed each other for years. The bar was nearly empty, a rainy weekday afternoon, and there was no music playing. While Soomin ordered us drinks, I went to the juke with a $5 bill, only realizing once I was there that picking the soundtrack was a lot of pressure on a first date. But I shook that off and played all the same songs I always played at that bar. I knew my selections almost by heart and started with Queen, then Nirvana, and down the line until I ran out of credits. "Killer Queen" blared while I punched in the rest of my selections, and right when I got back to the bar to take a seat next to Soomin, "Drain You" came on.

"This is my favorite Nirvana song!" he said, almost an accusation, a *how did you do that?* expression on his face.

"This is *my* favorite Nirvana song!" I replied, and we both laughed. Two years later we'd get a lyric from that song, "I'm lucky to've met you," engraved on our wedding rings.

I'd moved out of Leah's apartment on Avenue A and into a sunny little studio in Astoria, the first place I'd ever lived alone. I hung the dog masks above the front door, an owl drawing above my bed, and a neat row of smaller sculptures on a shelf, where I could stare at them through half-closed eyes as I fell asleep every night. On the wall behind the red couch was a timeline of my father's life and art made with color-coded index cards with notes about interviews and images. Soomin remarked on it once, asking if I was hunting a serial killer, and I gave him my canned explanation: My father was an artist and he died and I'm writing a book about him. I told him more about my father, and my writing, as he spent six nights a week there for almost a year and we cooked breakfast together and watched movies on my laptop in bed and told each other stories about our lives, pinpointing more and more moments and places where we might have walked right by each other for years.

While our experiences of the East Village were different (he came from the hard-working immigrant American Dream side of the neighborhood, as opposed to my punk-art iconoclast side), there was something deep and important that we shared: A fierce love for a neighborhood that was almost gone, but that we refused to give up. Gentrification had made the East Village nearly unrecognizable, but we both remembered a time when it was a community full of tough, creative people, not an amusement park for drunk frat boys. More importantly, we were both still able to see and cherish the parts of the old neighborhood that were left; the institutions that had managed to hold on through it all, the glimpses of home. One night, we went into Ray's Candy Store on Avenue A, where we'd both been going since we were little kids—and where I used to stop in every night during my hours of wandering to talk to Ray, the sweet old man who owned the place and had been working every night shift since the '70s. Ray greeted us excitedly, saying "I love her!" like he always did when I came in, and Soomin said "I do too!" and it felt like we were exactly where we were supposed to be.

Most of my old friends from the neighborhood had given up and left years ago, but I wasn't ready to let go and neither was Soomin. Eventually, we moved in together on Fifth Street, and a life started to take shape that had room for both my roots and a future.

I'd been thinking of stability as a high tower that I could build for myself, brick by brick, if only I could maintain enough focus and discipline. Something that had to be earned through sweat and sacrifice and constantly proving myself worthy and capable. Stability, I thought, was the prize for perfection, for becoming so utterly self-reliant that I could build myself an upper-middle-class life out of dirty scraps of nothing, through sheer force of will. It was a dream I was beginning to give up on, something that seemed impossible for a person as damaged as I felt.

A relationship with someone I actually trusted to catch me if I fell—someone who understood who I really was, not just who I was trying to be—introduced the possibility that maybe stability was something I could relax into. Maybe it wasn't about constantly striving until I successfully became a different person, but about creating a life with room to exhale. The idea that stability could be a state of calm, rather than a prize always just out of reach, was a revelation. And that it might actually be attainable for me was even more baffling.

My mother started dating Tom just a few months after she moved us out. At the time, I recognized him as an invader. I thought I hated him because he wasn't my father, but now I realize it was too soon to bring a third person into our freshly wounded lives when my mother and I were just learning how to be on our own together. If it had stayed just the two of us a little longer, we might have bonded, might have faced the world together, partners, like she always wanted us to be. But instead, Tom moved in and the living room became their bedroom. There was my room, and their room; no common space. Borders were drawn, walls were put up that never really came down.

Now though, she explained why Tom was so necessary. After we moved into the apartment on Lexington, she kept going to the methadone clinic and managed to get herself clean for real. She went regularly enough to earn the privilege of taking her methadone home, rather than having to take it at the clinic with a doctor watching. She took just as much as she needed to stave off withdrawal and hoarded the rest until she had enough to spend two weeks locked in the apartment, weaning herself off little by little, while I stayed with Stephanie and Jake.

"It was actually the most awful, awful thing in the world," she said. For weeks after the withdrawal was over she was still too weak and sick to get down the stairs of our apartment building. Always a small woman, she weighed just 93 pounds by the time she was done detoxing.

She said the temptation was there for a long time, but she only relapsed once, when she found a little chunk of heroin stuck to a piece of fabric after we'd moved again.

"What did you do with it?" I asked.

"Well," she said, laughing a little, "I smoked it!" Then she kind of trailed off as she elaborated, "I mean there it was. It wasn't possible for me not to. It really wasn't…" And I remembered that despite all of her success compared to my father, she was still struggling, still an addict, still fighting one of the hardest battles of will that a person can fight.

Tom's job transferred him from San Francisco to Carmel, and she begged him to take us with him. He was her ticket out, she explained, her escape hatch, insurance that she could stay clean.

"Living in the Mission, alone, still dancing," she said, "there's a chance I could have stayed clean. But there's a bigger chance I wouldn't have."

I didn't feel like I was escaping—I felt like I was being kidnapped. Now I know she was saving herself so she could save me, but that was beyond my grasp at eight years old. All I saw then was her sacrificing my home and family so we could go live with her boyfriend in a town that smelled like pine needles and money, the first place I'd ever lived that was quiet at night—a quiet that kept me awake as I strained into it listening for monsters, or at least the spiders that I knew must be everywhere.

When we were living in Carmel, I saw my father less and less. It went from every weekend to every other weekend, then once a month. It wasn't easy for my mother to ride the Greyhound bus with me back and forth every weekend when she was trying to build a life for us in a new town, and she didn't want to send me alone. But I don't think I even tried to pretend to care what was easy for her.

At my new school in Carmel, I told the teachers to call me Lilly Schactman, using my father's last name even though legally I'd always had my mother's because when I was born she still wasn't sure if he was going to stick around or not. I wanted it to be very clear, to her and to everyone else, whose side I'd chosen.

She told me that we were a family, she and I, and that families have to take care of each other. She told me we both had to make sacrifices, and asked me to be mature and grown up and to understand why things had to be the way they were. But her efforts to appeal to my sense of duty and empathy backfired. I understood them as an acknowledgment that she had uprooted my life for her well-being, chosen her happiness at the cost of mine. I continued to harden against her, a hardness that only started to soften when we dredged up all of this history together and I saw her as a recovering addict doing her best to protect her child, not just as my mother who never did quite enough.

The first year Soomin and I were dating, I brought him to my mother's house upstate for Thanksgiving. As we sat there scooping mashed potatoes, she regaled him with self-congratulatory tales of how she never made me eat food I didn't like when I was a kid and how that's so important, how she trusted me to make decisions for myself, like when I decided to stop going to high school.

I twitched a little as I watched her smile with pride, and him nod along politely. I buried my face in my wine glass, tempted to bite into it and let the shards fill my mouth as I stifled a tirade about how, in fact, she only admitted after the fact that I had been right about high school, and yes, it's true that she never made me finish my vegetables if I didn't want to, *but she was also a heroin addict.*

We never agreed on what our life together had looked like; what she was like as a mother, what I was like as a daughter, who was more at fault for so much friction. We'd never even really acknowledged that there was friction, that there was any blame to place—we'd just moved on from the explosive teenage years without ever exploring the damage.

If I had asked my mother for all of these details about my father and their past in a purely mother-daughter context, there's no way it would have been a calm, productive conversation. It would have been too raw for both of us, my wronged daughter-self lashing out at her flawed mother-self. She would have gotten defensive which would have made me push harder, until we weren't digging toward a truth together but just screaming our own grievances.

But now this wasn't about me and her directly. Now it was about the story, and I could ask her in my detached reporter voice, "What was that like?" even if underneath, what I meant was "How could you let this happen?" The structure of interviewing in service of storytelling kept us focused, pushing calmly ahead. I was collecting these moments of our lives, even the ugly ones, to build something out of them— like my father collected dead birds' wings and rusted springs. Not demanding apologies, just stories; just material.

We were taking the story down in chunks—years of this excavation, years of phone calls that opened with bracing questions, like, "When did you start using again in San Francisco?" and, "What was the last straw that ended your marriage?" But she never received these calls with hostility, or resistance, or even annoyance. She'd say, "Well!" and I could hear her settling into her chair and trying to put the words together carefully but truthfully.

I had been wary about interviewing my mother at first, had wanted to guard my project against the flood of her emotion. And she did overtake it in a way, but not the way I'd expected. As I started to understand her more and more through these stories, I realized I was shifting the landscape of my relationships with both of my parents, though I'd only set out to explore and shift one.

I realized somewhere along the way that whatever I wanted to call it—interviews, research—this was also me asking my mother all the questions that it otherwise wouldn't have occurred to me to ask her at all until she was dead too, and I went again searching desperately for something that was gone. I thought during some of these conversations, and between them, that I should appreciate them for what they were: not just traces of my father, but honest, intimate, past-plumbing conversations with my mother.

In the midst of all of this, I published an op-ed in a national paper about a viral photo of a little boy strapped into a car seat, staring into the camera, while his guardians sit nearly dead from opioid overdoses in the front seats. In the piece, I compared myself to that little boy and wrote about what it's like to be the child of addicts—all the feelings that had been churning around about how it's not their fault but it's still their responsibility, and how it creates a shame that's impossible not to inherit no matter how much you defend them, or how much you believe those defenses.

My mother called to tell me that when she first read the piece she was hurt, she wanted to argue, to point out that they never put me in that position. That most of the time they were just doing enough heroin to "maintain," to avoid withdrawal, that they weren't even really getting high, let alone doing enough to overdose. We were on the phone, so thankfully I didn't have to mask the mounting rage on my face as I held my tongue while she rationalized. But then, she said, she'd thought about it. She'd been rethinking a lot lately with all of these conversations we'd been having, and she'd realized that she'd convinced herself that because she did some things right, she had been a good mother. Or, the way I explained it back to her, her horrible childhood had set her bar for good parenting really, really low. By comparison, I had it great. I had two parents who loved me, who cared whether I was fed and safe, who played games and read me stories. She'd focused on that part, and pretended that growing up knowing my parents were addicts, watching it tear their marriage apart and destroy my father, somehow hadn't affected me.

I pressed the phone to my ear, overwhelmed, realizing how badly I'd needed to hear her say these things. I didn't interject; I just let her keep talking, repeating herself, explaining how her own perspective was shifting as we had all of these conversations and she was finally seeing that of course I had been harmed. Saying she was sorry.

Hearing her finally admit that she wasn't a perfect mother, that she let me be exposed to things no kid should know about, that she'd let me fend for my own emotional wellbeing when I most needed her help—hearing her apologize—cracked something open in me. I'd wanted for years to throw all of this in her face, to accuse her, to expose her. But as soon as she admitted it, all I felt was forgiveness.

Soomin and I decided to get married while spending a weekend on Fire Island. There was no big surprise proposal, but a long conversation late at night, sitting on the patio of our motel with a bottle of white wine in a bucket of ice, talking about what we both wanted out of the future. We looked out over the quiet, carless street, dotted with fireflies and ringing with cricket chirps, and talked about every important thing we could think of that we'd need to agree on before committing to a life together. It felt like the world was ours and we could make it into whatever we wanted.

We talked about kids, how many we wanted (agreeing on at least one and no more than three), and the fact that the first one of any gender would have to be named Joseph or Jo for my father. I told him I was probably never going to make any real money as a writer, and that had to be ok. He said he was going to run businesses, that he had big ambitions, but that meant he'd have to work a lot, especially in the beginning. I said great, I'll have to work a lot too.

Back in the city, when wedding planning was in full swing, I made a list of the few traditional things we might want to include. We were doing away with most of the pomp, keeping it nice and simple, but we still wanted to cut a big cake together, share a first dance to a song we could forever refer to as "our wedding song," a couple of the basics. As I scrawled out the list, the logical next tradition up for debate was the father-daughter and mother-son dances that usually come after the couple's first dance. I had, of course, thought about my father's absence at the wedding before this moment. But, sitting at an outdoor table at one of my favorite East Village restaurants on a warm summer evening with a glass of wine, writing in the notebook that was specifically designated for wedding-related lists, my pen hovered above the blank line, and the reality set in.

I looked up and down Eighth Street, like I was looking for some indication that this was real, that I was really going to get married without my father there, that he wouldn't even know it was happening. I was 27 years old, but looking around like a little kid lost at the grocery store. I looked back down at the notebook page, "cake, best man/maid of honor speeches, first dance," and tried to imagine my father there—not even walking me down an aisle; I would settle for just seeing him sitting quietly in a corner of the venue in a button-down shirt he would have bought just for the occasion, and his scuffed work boots, smiling at me in that way of his that crinkled the skin around his eyes so much you almost couldn't see them anymore. Then I let myself imagine us dancing together, resting my head on his shoulder like I used to when I fell asleep while we were out and he'd carry me home. And then I had to get the check before I started bawling, alone at my little table next to a couple just trying to enjoy their early dinner.

Walking the three blocks home down Avenue A, along the edge of the park, I seriously considered scrapping the reception all together. As soon as I was safely in the hallway of our building on Fifth Street, the tears I'd been holding in poured out, and by the time I made it up to the fourth floor, I was messy, loud, gasp-crying. I opened the apartment door and Soomin was standing in the kitchen. He froze with a cracker in one hand and a butter knife with cheese on it in the other, looking up at me full of concern, bracing for terrible news, unsure what was happening. I went into our bedroom and collapsed onto the bed, and when he followed and lay down next to me, asking what had happened, I explained in a rambling, high-pitched flood how much it hurt to do this without my father. How I didn't want to do it without him, how I felt like I was leaving him behind, betraying him, by standing up in front of everyone I knew and saying I was happy. That to get married felt like saying I had what I needed in life, that I was ready to go forward and into a new future, but how could I do that? How could I ignore the fact that my father was gone and my life was missing so much?

I'd talked to Soomin about my father a lot, told him stories and showed him pictures and artwork, but this was the first time I'd cried for my father in front of him. It happened so rarely now, my grief an ever-present, low thrum rather than swells that sloshed their way out as tears. But the prospect of getting married without my father there was too much. It was everything I'd been dreading since he died: a life without him, full of big, defining moments that he should be there for. Once again, I was faced with the feeling that by living my life, I was abandoning my father, that each milestone I reached brought me further and further away from him.

Soomin didn't try to talk me out of how I was feeling, just lay there with me while I cried. "We can do whatever you want to do," he said.

But I knew that no matter how much it hurt, I couldn't let my father's absence prevent me from celebrating what I did have. As central as my grief is to who I am, I couldn't let it overshadow the fact that I'd found someone to be happy with, someone who made me excited about the future. I knew my father wouldn't want me to, either. I used to think that staying rooted in my grief was a way of honoring my father, a vigil I would hold for the rest of my life. But after so many years of writing about my father and spending time in my memories of him, I knew that would break his heart.

I started to come around to the idea that a better way to honor my father would be to live a life he'd be happy to see me living. He wanted so much for me. While his marriage was falling apart, he was worried about the example my parents were setting for me because he wanted me to believe in love. He wanted to be a better man and a better father so that I could have a good life and grow up able to trust. He would want me to be happy, with or without him.

So I let myself have a good cry about how unfair it was that my father would miss my wedding, raging at him for missing it and at the permanence of death. I felt sorry for myself as I lay in bed and let Soomin curl his body around mine. And then I sniffled and said that of course I still wanted a wedding reception. I would even wear white.

After my mother and I moved out, my father couldn't afford a place of his own with his income divided between child support (when he paid it) and heroin, so he slept on a lot of couches. One of those couches belonged to Audrey Newell, a friend of his from Academy Studios where they worked together making natural history museum displays and carpooled from San Francisco to the studio in Novato, about an hour drive.

I liked Audrey when I was a kid. She had short red hair and a big black poodle named Lucifer and lots of stuff in her apartment was bright pink and lime green. I hadn't seen her since that day before my father's funeral when I hid in her bedroom from everyone's whispers. I called her and asked her to tell me what she remembered about my father. She told me about the carpool, about how my father was the only member who never took a turn driving. He didn't have a car or a license, so really he just hitched.

Audrey remembered how bad he smelled then, with his addiction worse than ever and no wife around to beg him to clean himself. He didn't bathe or change his socks, and his teeth were turning brown. She said other people in the carpool pushed her to tell him he had to start bathing or stop riding with them. She brought it up with him a few times and he just shrugged and mumbled. He didn't care at all what people thought of him at work. If he hadn't showered to avoid repulsing the woman he loved, he certainly wasn't going to do it so his coworkers would have a more pleasant ride to work. He probably thought they were stuck up.

Audrey told me they fought a lot when he stayed with her. She didn't want him doing drugs in her house, and often noticed cash missing. "I was so furious with him when you were there over the weekends and I could tell he was high," she told me, her voice cracking a little.

She said that she was never sure if he actually liked her or if he just didn't want to have to take a bus to work every day. She was not holding back. She was telling me all the little angry private thoughts that she had then, that she'd held onto. She was telling me what she really thought of my father, like I'd been trying to get everyone to do. But now I felt defensive of him, suspicious that she was exaggerating, romanticizing the idea of having known a junkie once in her own artist heyday.

Audrey described what she called his 'lair,' a little hovel tucked away in the corner of the Academy Studios warehouse where he would collect scraps of leftover materials and periodically hide to work on his own projects.

"He treated it like his personal art supply store," Audrey said. "He stole so much stuff!"

He used to smuggle out supplies for us to play with: little Ziploc bags full of incredibly lifelike fake eyes, plaster molds of lizard scales, scraps of fake fur. It was one of the things that made him magical, pockets always full of treasure.

Audrey was convinced that if anyone else had collected piles of trash in the work site and then disappeared in the middle of the day to play with them, they would've been fired. She thought the bosses must've known he was doing heroin at work but looked the other way because sometimes when he was high he would just put his headphones on and draw, focusing more completely than anyone else there. And he did such beautiful work.

Audrey choked up as she told me about the time she finally got up the nerve to ask him something she'd wondered about for a while.

"I looked right at him," she said, "and I asked if he ever made art when he was sober. His eyes went down to the ground, then up to the sky. Eventually he said 'no.'"

After I hung up the phone with Audrey I lay on my bed for a long time. I stared up at the papier-mâché bird skeleton sculpture, one of my favorite pieces. It's made of pages ripped from my father's notebooks, so his words spiral around the bird's ribs, mirror-shard feathers hanging off of it like voodoo icicles. I stared at it, Audrey's words replaying in my head, thinking about whether it was true that his art was inextricably tied to his addiction—that this part of him that I cherished so much, that I clung to, was a byproduct of what killed him.

I thought, for the first time, about what it would have been like if he had lived and kept using. In all of my imagined scenarios of what it could have been like if he'd lived, I had always imagined him clean and healthy. My mother has kept that part of her life behind her, and I always took it for granted that he would have, too, if he were still here. But if he couldn't make art without heroin, there's no way he would have stayed clean.

If he'd lived, would I have ended up another name on the long list of people whose couches he claimed for a little longer than he was welcome, covering them in sawdust, filling the room with his stench? Would he have stolen from me? Would I have let him get away with it? I've never doubted that my life would be better if he was still here, but I started to wonder about the different ways his presence could have hurt me almost as much as his absence.

It was horrible to think about, this alternate reality where he lived and I grew to hate him. I looked up at the bird skeleton and I was momentarily disgusted by it.

But then I snapped out of it.

There may have been a period in my father's life, at the depth of his addiction, when he honestly believed that he couldn't make art without heroin. He may have told Audrey as much. But it was bullshit. And if he had lived, I would have told him it was bullshit. *Artist* was so much closer to the core of him than *junkie*. The ideas, the images, the symbols, the skill all came from him, from his brilliant mind. They weren't injected into him along with the drugs. Heroin might've helped him get into the mind-state to make art, it might have slowed his demons down enough that he could catch them and turn them into sculpture, but he would have found another way into the work.

I wanted to smack him for ever thinking that those beautiful things came from drugs, not from him. And I thought for the first time about how much knowing me as an adult could have helped him, not just how much it could have helped me.

Opposite: Detail

Papier-mâché (notebook pages),
painted mirror shards; 19″

Blood and ink on paper

Another thing Audrey said that struck me as strange was, "I hope you have some positive memories of him." It took me a moment to realize what she meant, because I have almost exclusively positive memories of him. I have the fondest memory of playing catch in the hallway of the Donnelly Hotel, an SRO on Market Street where he lived after he burned through the friends who were willing to let him crash on their couches. The carpet was the color and texture of fungus, the lighting was dim, the ancient wallpaper peeling off in strips. My father stood at one end of the hallway, next to the reception desk, which was surrounded with bullet-proof glass. I stood at the other end, near the stairs that led up to the rooms that could be rented by the hour, night, or week.

I was nine, and completely unfazed. As we tossed the tennis ball back and forth, my father would make exaggerated sounds of strain as he lunged to catch my "fastballs," and cheer me on when I caught his. It was our version of the most wholesome trope there is.

"I was ready to fucking murder him," my mother said, still fuming almost twenty years later about the time he left me alone in his room there. "It was a fucking crack hotel! Who knows what could have happened."

At the time, I wanted every last moment I could get with him, and I didn't care what her reasoning was for not wanting me to stay there. I didn't care that the light bulbs in the hallways buzzed and the room smelled funky and there were sometimes people slumped over, nodding out in the hallways. Her anger makes sense now. I wouldn't want any kid of mine (or even any friend of mine) to stay in a place like that. But as a child I didn't see or understand the danger. The truth is, while it took my mother a long time to realize that their addictions had damaged me, it took me a long time too.

I had a happy childhood, and my parents were junkies. Both of these things are true.

I have my father's soft and faded Sun Records shirt that still, after all these years, smells like him. Sometimes when I'm really missing him, I bury my face in that shirt and take a deep breath. To me it doesn't smell like a junkie, but like my Papa.

After talking to Audrey and my mother about how strung out and filthy he was then, when he didn't look out of place at the Donnelly and smelled so bad people didn't want to be in a car with him, I took the shirt out of my drawer and held it up to my nose. I wondered if these new images of the man who wore it would change how I felt about the smell. I balled the shirt up and stuck my nose in it, taking a deep breath. Then I breathed in even deeper, trying to get as much of the smell as possible as I was flooded with memories of running to hug my Papa at a bus stop after I hadn't seen him in weeks, of sitting in his studio with him while he told me stories about his favorite painters and we giggled about puns, of lying with my head on his chest, the rise and fall of his breath rocking me to sleep as he read me Greek myths.

I was reminded of standing outside of the Loft, of knowing that the vast, magical place I remembered could not physically fit inside of the normal-sized building I was looking at. And I realized that I'd been thinking of the two realities—the one I remember and the one that adults around me saw happening—as in irreconcilable conflict with each other. I'd been thinking of truth as something stronger than memory, something that could—and even should—erase what I remembered if they didn't match up. I thought that if I shone a light on all of these demons that had been lurking in the shadows of my childhood, I would tear myself out of illusion and into the brightness of reality. But the more I heard about the lowest points in my father's life—about how he appeared, from the outside—the more I realized that this reality wasn't any stronger than the one in my memory. I may have been able to learn more about who he was as a man, but even the ugliest truths wouldn't change who he was to me as my father.

Regardless of what was going on in those rooms, the hallway of the Donnelly Hotel was great for a game of catch. And that smell that repulsed everyone else triggers only happy memories for me. I keep the shirt wrapped up tight to preserve the smell, but I wish I could use it as a pillowcase and bury my face in it while I sleep, to dream of my father.

Ink drawing of Lilly on a swing, in the playground near the Donnelly Hotel

Eventually, Joe must have been so obvious about being high at work that his bosses at Academy Studios could no longer ignore it. They gave him a choice: lose his job, or go to rehab. They offered to pay, and he accepted. Saving up the money for inpatient treatment had been impossible on his own—if he ever managed to stash away more than a few bucks, he either felt guilty and gave it to my mother as child support, or he caved and spent it on drugs. This was a chance he wouldn't have been able to get any other way.

With the help of a treatment program, he was finally able to put together those seven clean days in a row he'd always been reaching for, and then a bunch more—one day at a time, as they say.

After years of heavy, tortured work, he started making delicate, fresh things. This, to me, is the biggest barometer that he was making real progress. He drew birds sitting calmly outside of cages—the cages often depicted as a woman's delicate, tented fingers. He made a tiny book, with pages no more than one-inch-by-one-inch, called "The Bird-in-Hand Book," with a different drawing of a bird in a hand, modeled after his own, on each page. In some they were caged, but in most they perched, free and content. He'd used dead bird wings in his sculptures for years, and made flightless angels with concrete wings, but now there were birds in flight, birds as freedom.

He made silverpoint "pens" himself, by splitting the end of a pencil-sized stick, sliding in a very thin piece of silver wire, and fixing it with glue and cruder copper wire. He would use a jeweler's magnifying glass, holding it in place with a squint, to draw finely detailed figures on pieces of found bone. The lines were so thin and light they looked like they were naturally part of the bones, almost blending in with the small fissures. The effect was as if tiny, pristine figures were slowly appearing on the decaying bones, emerging out of them as if from under the surface of still water. Clean.

Silverpoint on bone
fragment, approx. 1″
(enlarged to show detail)

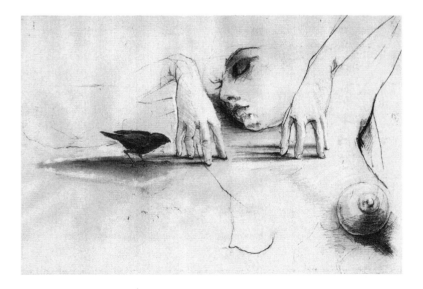

Top: Woodcut on paper

Bottom: Drawing/study for woodcut

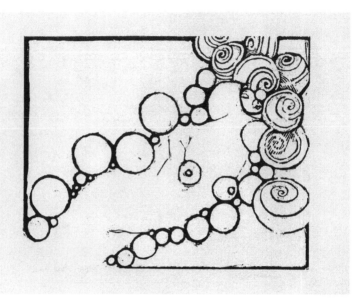

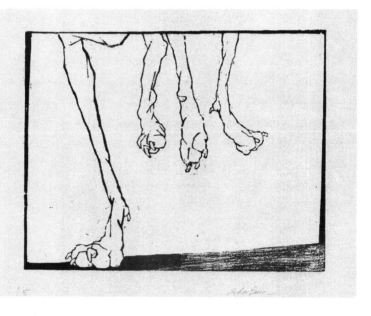

Top: Woodcut on paper
(Note: A copy of this print hangs in Mona's bar, a gift from the author)

Bottom: Woodcut on paper

I know he must have felt confident about his recovery, because he even tried to reconcile with his father. Their relationship had been strained for a long time, and it got worse when Amy told Barry about her brother's addiction, when my parents' marriage was falling apart and they were no longer able to pretend nothing was wrong. Amy didn't know what to do, watching her brother sink further and further into heroin darkness, and she hoped their dad might be able to help. Barry offered to pay for rehab, but only if Joe came home to St. Louis. Of course, he refused. After that Barry never considered it worth his time to talk to his son, even harshly. I got letters and boxes of books from my grandfather on birthdays and Hannukah, but nothing came for my father. The letters didn't even mention him.

When he started putting his life back together, Joe tried reaching out to his father several times, writing to Amy about his efforts, "considering the absolute low point his feelings about me have (must have) reached, there is so little to lose." But he was also paralyzed by the knowledge that his efforts would probably be rejected. "I've now written him 27 pages, not counting the letter that I did send," he wrote. He continued to try even after Barry started returning his letters, unopened.

He also started going to synagogue, finding religion for the first time in his life. He would bring me with him on Friday nights as the official start to our weekends together, usually followed by a banana split at Baskin Robins. (Every time, he'd ask, "Wanna split a banana split?")

Now that he was no longer a young nomad, hitchhiking to Mexico for fun and living out some ramblin' man fantasy, but an untethered, approaching-middle-aged man who had lost his family and couldn't afford a place to live, it was suddenly important to him to have heritage. When we started going to temple, his family wasn't just a dead mother, a father who wouldn't speak to him, a sister who lived far away, a wife who had left him, and a daughter he lived in constant fear of disappointing—it was thousands of years of history.

Until then, I had a vague understanding that I was Jewish insofar as I was not Christian and I was apparently required to enjoy rye bread. But now we were going to temple every week, and my father was trying to teach me about my own Jewishness by showing me *Fiddler on the Roof* and reading to me from the Old Testament. Since we only got two days a week together now at most, everything we did together, everything that was just ours, became even more important. Being Jewish was something that he and I shared, that my mother wasn't a part of. It was a bond that he wanted to strengthen, to make me as much his daughter as possible.

We studied the prayers together, learning Hebrew pronunciation. When we looked at the translated versions that all started with "Blessed are you, lord our God" and I asked him if he believed in God, he responded with, "Good question. Do you?"

He didn't want to taint my answer with his own, he wanted me to really consider the question for myself. This had the benefit of allowing me to come to my own conclusions about God and religion, but it also means I never found out how much he really believed. If I could ask him again now, I wonder if he would give me a straight answer or if he'd again answer the question with a question.

I treated the Old Testament like every other book of myths he had read to me during my childhood, illustrating it while he read aloud. I tried to make paper dolls of every person mentioned, but gave up at the "begot" section. Watching *Fiddler on the Roof* made me feel Jewish more than the Torah did, in that it introduced me to the troubled history of our people and made me feel a deep sadness for it, and it gave me an appreciation for the comedic potential of overly analytical elders. It also resulted in months and months of my father randomly breaking into song while walking down the street, belting "If I Were a Rich Man," his spot-on imitation of Tevye made even funnier by his slim frame and the chain that attached his wallet to his keys jangling loudly as he shook his body back and forth.

Once, when we were at Temple Shareth Beth Israel and the congregation was standing for the Kaddish, the prayer for the dead, I heard him whisper "Phyllis Rita Schactman" during the pause to say the names of loved ones. I looked up at him, aware that I was witnessing an important moment of vulnerability as I saw him blink away a tear while praying for his mother. I knew she'd died before I was born and that he loved her, but I'd never really understood that he still missed her, unfamiliar with the idea of lifelong grief.

In a letter to Amy he wrote of being a Jew, "I've learned it's like being an artist, it's a process, a become-ing, a state of become-ing. More of a verb than a noun." Both the artistic and the spiritual drive are a constant effort to do better, either to create better art or to make oneself into a better person, to get closer to inspiration or closer to God, a parallel that he found irresistible.

He went on in the letter to explain that he had found, "no answers, but, as w/ anything that teaches, a deepen-ing/sharpen-ing of the question(ing)(s)." By his definition, my quest to understand him as a person was right in line with his quests to understand art and God—no satisfactory answers would ever be found, but the searching, the deepening and sharpening of the questions, is what carries the inquisitive, creative mind through life—and it's what keeps a relationship alive with someone who's not.

That something he wrote so accurately described this project of mine made me feel that I was doing it right. It also made me feel a little better about the fact that even as I learned more and more about my father's life, he was still a silhouette to me; I could tell his whole life story, and he still wouldn't be here to keep living it.

When I started getting serious about turning this project into something I could someday publish, I read one memoir after another, studying the way they were put together with a drive and curiosity that

I hadn't felt since I was a teenager reading *The Master and Margarita* in the park, determined to educate myself better than Bard could. When I read Lidia Yuknavitch's *The Chronology of Water*, it blew open my ideas about what a personal story can be and do like nothing had since Anaïs Nin. I walked around for days with the story and the water imagery swirling around in my mind before realizing the most important difference between Lidia and Anaïs in the pantheon of writers I love: Lidia is alive. I could talk to her, maybe even learn from her. I looked her up online and discovered that she taught weekend-long writing workshops in Portland, and started saving for airfare immediately.

The first day of the workshop, Lidia explained that she believes every writer has a handful of core metaphors in their life and their writing that they can always return to for new meaning, symbols that reverberate deep within us as an endless well of inspiration and material—one of hers being water. I thought immediately of my father's work and his core metaphors of dogs, deer, and rabbits that he returned to over and over and over, and knew that he would likely agree, and would have something so smart to add, if only I could write him a letter about this workshop.

Lidia then told the group of us, about twenty writers sitting around a table in her writing center in downtown Portland, to make a list of our own core metaphors, the imagery that keeps pulling us back. And I was stumped. I could only think of my father's metaphors. The imagery I'd been writing about for years was all his: his dogs, his deer, his rabbits. But did that make them mine, too, because I'd been writing about them for so long? Or did I not have any metaphors of my own, because I'd been too busy writing into someone else's imagery to develop my own?

Then I realized with an audible gasp that caused several writers to look up from their own lists, that by weaving this time traveling spell of the story of my father, I was not just decoding his symbols, I was inheriting them. Of course they were mine too, not just to observe and read, but to play with, to make my own meaning out of. I didn't just inherit the physical pieces of his artwork; I inherited the language in which his art was written, like I'd hoped to do all along. I'd tiptoed around the edges of this knowledge, thinking about the book I was writing as my own continuation of his Hunter/Hunted series as I chased my father's story into the core of my own grief, thinking of writing about him as a response to the call of his work, but it was bigger than that. I wasn't just layering his imagery into my own creative experience, but building my own identity as an artist out of the pieces my father had left behind for me.

As I found my footing as a writer, I wanted more than ever to have my father around to talk to—about the creative life, about the ideas that possessed us and the practical challenges of functioning in society when all you want to do is work. But even in his absence, maybe especially in his absence, my father had helped me find my voice and build my own creative practice through the telling of his story, the project I devoted the first decade of my adulthood to.

When I was seven, I drew a princess and proudly presented it to my father. I'd spent a long time creating the finely detailed pattern on her big puffy skirt and the spikes on her crown were impressively tall, almost as tall as she was. She was undeniably regal. He studied the drawing for a moment, holding it away from his face and squinting one eye just like he did when he considered a piece of his own work before deciding whether it was finished. Looking back at me, he asked why I'd drawn the figure so small. "Use the whole page," he said, before handing the drawing back. "Don't forget about your negative space."

He was reminding me of an earlier lesson about how the paper you leave blank has its own shape, just like whatever you draw, and they define each other by their contrast. One can't exist without the other, so the shape of the absence is just as important as the shape of the figure.

I had built my life, and then my art, around the shape of my father's absence. Even in death, my father was still teaching me how to be an artist.

Top: "Transcript:" Woodcut on paper

Bottom: "For the Word-Cave:" Woodcut on paper

In the summer of 1999, Academy Studios sent Joe to Chicago to do an installation. He'd been clean for several months—the only clean period I could truly verify because he'd agreed to drug testing as a condition of keeping his job after completing the rehab program they sent him to. But in a new city, away from home, away from supervision, the temptation was too great. While he was in Chicago, he was arrested and charged with possession of heroin.

While we were waiting to find out what would happen to him, it all finally started to hit me—the full truth of what I'd only vaguely understood before. I was eleven then, old enough to grasp in a more tangible sense what it meant that my father was an addict. What it could mean. I had nightmares about talking to him through glass, about sitting next to him and not being able to hear him. Nightmares about him being taken away. I'd seen enough movies and gotten enough lectures at school by this point to understand that he was doing something dangerous, that I should be angry and scared, and that something bad was probably going to happen to him. I'd scolded the D.A.R.E. representative that came to my school for making it sound like addicts were all bad people. But even as I yelled "You don't know what you're talking about!" and went to the bathroom to cry, I also internalized some of their messages: drugs were bad, and if you did drugs, you were hurting yourself and your family.

Instead of going to prison, my father ended up in court-ordered rehab. All I remember from talking to him on the phone when he was there was that he told me about a friend he'd made, that people there liked him because he could do perfect impressions of counselors and other patients, and made them laugh even when they were locked away and sick. He managed to make it sound like sleep-away camp, even while he was going through the physical misery of withdrawal, and the indignity of it being against his will.

Back in New York, he stayed with Joni, Cathy's older sister with whom he'd remained close friends, and who had helped him out financially many, many times over the years. But she kicked him out when he stole money from her son's piggybank. Then he stayed with Chris Harvey, the friend who helped pay our rent in Williamsburg, before anyone knew why my parents were having trouble coming up with the money. Once again, my father was bouncing around, crashing with friends, but now it was less Jack Kerouac and more King Lear; where once he could play it off as part of a lifestyle, it was clear now that this was instability, not freedom.

Chris was always one of my favorite of my father's friends. I remember telling Papa when I was about four that I liked Chris because he didn't talk to me like I was a baby like some other grown-ups did. "Because he's not *condescending*," my father rephrased for me—and I always remember that exchange as how I learned the word.

Chris came over to my place, and after we made some small talk and caught up, he told me about driving my father around the city, looking for an apartment. He had almost no money and terrible credit, so the only places he could look at were small, dingy, depressing studios in bad neighborhoods.

"I started to think the whole thing was a bad idea," Chris said, explaining that it would be really hard to stay clean living in a dilapidated studio with junkies and dealers in the building and on the corner. One hand on my orange tabby's back, petting her distractedly, Chris told me he called his uncle Dede, who had been an addiction counselor for years, to ask for advice about how to help Joe. Dede told Chris that Joe needed three things: the love of a close family elder, physical labor to keep him busy, and nature—or what he called "a piece of the sky."

Chris asked if he had any older relatives he was close to, and Joe told him about his Aunt Rhoda, Barry's sister, who happened to live in the redwoods of Northern California—with a big piece of the sky.

He told me Joe didn't put up much of a fight when he suggested that he go stay with Rhoda. "He kind of grumbled about not wanting to go back to California," Chris said, "but pretty much in the same breath he said he knew it was a good idea."

Rhoda arranged a place for him to stay in the woods outside of the tiny town of Redway where it would be difficult to get his hands on heroin, and got him a job building log cabins. A family elder, nature, and physical labor to keep him busy. Chris brought him to the airport and arranged for Rhoda to pick him up. "Bring him straight to the woods," he recalled telling her, "and keep him there."

The first cabin he built was the tiny one that he would live in, on the property that belonged to Rhoda's pot-farming friends Berle and Sherie.

He called Chris every few weeks, never acknowledging that he was checking in, but finding excuses as obscure as Jack London's birthday to call "just to say hi," and to mention that he was doing well, that he was healthy—using the same code for clean that he used with me.

He sent me postcards of the beautiful redwood forests, and we planned a camping trip for that September. We'd been camping once, in Big Sur when I was very little, but now I was finally old enough for a real father-daughter camping trip. We'd collect art supplies in the woods, and sit by the fire and carve. He would tell me about his time camping with Mark and Brian and Ken, that formative trip where the deer imagery was born. I wrote him a letter in lavender gel pen full of exclamation points, all about how excited I was to see him, and he sent me letters and postcards at least once a week, full of plans and drawings, telling me how beautiful it was there and how much fun we were going to have when I came to visit.

There was a new lightness in his voice when we talked on the phone, an excitement and a clarity, as crisp as the fresh air he was breathing. He was healthy, for real.

When he'd been living in Redway a few months, my mother took me to spend the weekend with him in San Francisco, and he took the bus down to meet us there. My parents hadn't said a civil word to each other since they split up four years earlier, but somehow we managed to have a perfect weekend together, the three of us. We ate ice cream as we walked around the Mission, circuitously avoiding walking past the house with the basketball hoop and the garage, the last place we'd all lived together. Nobody acknowledged how far away those days felt, but looking back I'm sure we all thought it. It was like we were walking around the outside edges of our old life, never quite going back in, but brushing up against it now and then. I gave my father his birthday present—a little plastic box of seashells, a miniature starfish, and a fossilized shark tooth—and he cradled it in his hands like it was full of precious jewels, giving me a big hug and an enthusiastic "Wow! Thank you, Lilly!" The cold zipper of his leather jacket pressed into my face and I inhaled a deep breath of stale cigarette smoke and pencil shavings.

As we turned the corner from 16th Street onto Valencia, we spotted the outside sale rack of our favorite used bookstore—I don't know its actual name; we used to call it "Kafka and Hank's," for the two store cats—my father and I agreed with a glance that we'd have to go in. My mother had been married to him for long enough to know that there was no such thing as just walking past a bookstore once he'd peered inside. Without a word, we filed between the two big display windows and in through the heavy black door, which my father held for us both. And for a heartbeat's worth of time, we were a family again.

I went straight for Hank, the fluffier and more outgoing of the two cats, who was sitting on the "staff picks" table right inside the door, scratching him behind the ears as the door slammed shut behind us. It was always a little dark in there, creating a cozy, living room feeling that the cats only amplified. My mother went left, browsing clockwise, her dyed-auburn hair falling between her shoulder blades as she looked up at the high shelves, running her silver-laden fingers idly along the books' spines. My father made a straight line toward the back-right corner where the big glossy art books were. By the time I'd found Kafka napping under a table toward the back and we were all ready to go, my father headed to the register with a hardcover copy of Phillip Pullman's *The Golden Compass*—which I'd forgotten telling him weeks earlier that I wanted to read.

Then we went to Hamburger Mary's, where I made my milkshake last as long as I could before we said goodbye, and my father wrote me a letter on his bus ride home, warning me not to let adolescence shrink me, telling me to stand up and be proud, and apologizing for everything he'd put me through in the last few years.

We talked on the phone one afternoon a few weeks later and he said he wasn't feeling great, that he was going to lie down and take a nap. He never woke up.

My mother told me I didn't have to go with her to pack up my father's things if I didn't want to. I could stay at the motel in Redway with Amy and she would take care of it, but when I said I wanted to go, she understood. Packing up his room would be my last physical interaction with him, my last chance to be surrounded by his smell, to see exactly what he had seen before he closed his eyes for the last time. I wanted to lie down on the bed where he'd died and mix my tears with the last traces of him.

On the drive out into the woods, I wondered what would be sitting on his night table, the last things he had seen and touched. Probably a book, but which one? A new favorite art postcard? Maybe a letter he was in the middle of writing to me. His most recent drawings and prints would be hanging on the wall so he could live with them for a while and decide if they were any good.

As we turned the corner of the dirt road onto Berle and Sherie's property, up to the little cabin he'd been living in—that he'd died in—we saw a stack of boxes in the driveway. I didn't understand at first, but as it became clear that they'd already packed everything up for us, I became frantic, furious. I was too shocked to cry, and I don't remember anything else after seeing the pile of boxes—so sterile and unceremonious.

The first morning at the motel in Redway, just a few days after he died, I woke up in a darkened room on scratchy, pilled sheets. My mouth was dry and my eyes were swollen. I could see an empty bed next to the one I was in and I could tell that there was bright sun shining outside of the drawn curtains. It could have been seven in the morning or three in the afternoon. First, I remembered I was in California. Then I remembered why. During that first week, there were a few seconds every morning before I was fully awake when I thought it had all been a dream.

As I sat up, it felt like someone was dragging their fingernails along the inside of my skull; I was dehydrated from so much crying. The motel carpet felt simultaneously rough and worn under my bare feet. I didn't bother to change out of the large t-shirt that went past my knobby twelve-year-old knees, or to tie back my long curly hair that had been worked into a Bride of Frankenstein crown by several nights of tossing and turning through sweaty nightmares.

As I opened the door, I was almost knocked backward by the brightness of the sun. It dried my eyeballs to match the sandy texture inside my mouth. I hoped maybe I would faint.

Everyone from our group was sitting by the pool, a few yards from the door I was stepping out of—my mother, Amy, my father's old friend Myra and her daughter, Lily, and maybe a couple of others. As I stood there blinking in the sun, waiting for my eyes to focus on anything other than bright whiteness, they all stopped talking and turned to look at me. The focus of their concerned eyes made me nauseous. I was already so at sea; I couldn't stand the extra pressure of feeling like I was on display and expected to act a certain way. *What does heartbreak look like?* I wondered. *What do they want from me?*

I took a step backward and closed the door, neon red spots floating in my eyes from the shock of the sun. I dug through the suitcase I didn't remember packing and pulled out the bathing suit I definitely hadn't thought to bring. My mother must have known there was a pool at the motel. I wondered how she could keep track of such details at a time like this, but was glad she had. My bathing suit was a bright purple one-piece, associated with a light-hearted joy that I couldn't even register as a familiar emotion in that moment. I'd worn it to play on the beach, running away from crashing waves and getting sunburned. Today, I would wear it to hide.

I opened the door again. Not pausing this time, I walked straight toward the pool. I kept my eyes fixed on the shimmering blue water, not looking up toward the group that I knew was staring at me again. I didn't respond as the black asphalt seared the bottoms of my bare feet, didn't look up as my mother let out a gentle, "Hi, sweetheart," like a sigh.

I had never learned to swim, but I jumped into the kidney-shaped pool anyway. The shock of the cold water brought me closer to fully conscious than I had been in days. I briefly considered just inhaling that cold water into my lungs and going away, but I held my breath instead. As I closed my eyes and focused on how the water muffled every sound, I felt the first moment of relief. I knew they were all still out there, with their "poor thing"s and their "can I get you anything?"s, but in the pool, underwater, suspended, I was somewhere else, alone, away from the motel and outside of time.

There was a small memorial service at the home of a hippie woman rabbi—there would be two larger services later, one in New York and one in San Francisco, but this was the intimate one. When we were settled, only about ten of us sitting on folding chairs in a circle in this stranger's living room, the rabbi started singing "Swing Low, Sweet Chariot." My mother, my aunt Amy, and I all made eye contact, the way you look at a friend in school when a teacher says something they don't realize could be an innuendo. We were all remembering Papa singing "Swing Low, Sweet Chariot," in an impossibly loud baritone, with the same boisterous spirit with which he sang the Mighty Mouse theme song, or "If I Were a Rich Man," or "Stop in the Name of Love"—for no reason other than a laugh—while walking down the street.

We all tried to remain serious and respectful, keeping our eyes on the ground. I don't remember who broke first, but by the time the rabbi reached the first chorus we were all laughing hysterically, almost falling off of our chairs, fresh tears streaming down our cheeks as we imagined him rolling his eyes.

I don't remember this part, but years later Lily told me she remembers the rabbi asking what was funny, and me saying, "It's just that…my father would hate this."

I wanted to stand up and speak. As I swam back and forth across the pool, images had floated into my mind of me dressed in black, with sunlight filtering through the redwoods Papa and I would never get our chance to camp under, reflecting off of my golden hair, which I would make sure to brush before then. I imagined that I would say something wise and mature and it would make everyone feel stupid for acting like I was a child who didn't understand their whispers about how it must have been an overdose that killed him. I would say something touching and true, and everyone would cry. It would be a tragic, beautiful moment. But then, sitting in a circle in the rabbi's little cabin, the time came and I couldn't push the air out to speak. I knew I'd never be able to sufficiently express everything my father had meant to me.

Initially when I started the search that would become this book, I thought I was giving myself a clearer picture of what to mourn, but instead I created a way to stay close to my father that was separate from mourning. For a decade, I surrounded myself with his work, his letters, his friends, chasing down traces of him, dancing with him like a hunter with a deer, a hero with his monster, an artist with her subject. And in doing so I found a way for him to be a part of my life again; not just his absence, but him—his art, his relationships, his mannerisms and memories. I kept my life tethered to him as long as he was the question I was trying to answer.

My father would have loved nothing more than to be the subject of one of the big art books he used to pore over in bookstores—and for a while that's what I thought I was writing. But this became something different—not just a record of his work that will live on when the wood sculptures have rotted and the metal pieces come apart from their bases, but the conversations we never got to have, a new chapter of our relationship.

If he had lived, I wouldn't have written this book. In a strange way, I might not feel as close to him as I do now, his life and story and art such an urgent thread in my life. I hold the image of us together, artist-father and writer-daughter drinking coffee, talking craft and words and life, so tightly that I can almost see it like a photograph. But it's an image that would be impossible even if he'd lived—the version of me that I became without him could never have known him. They can only exist together here on these pages, and in my mind. I wonder sometimes what will happen when I'm finally done with this book, when I don't have this search to keep me connected to him anymore. I expect that I'll mourn him all over again, in a whole new way.

Recently, Soomin and I went to Amsterdam, and I stood in Rembrandt's studio and cried. It feels good to cry about Papa now; it happens so much less frequently than in the early years when it was always just under the surface. When it happens now, I'm surprised and relieved to see that I can still feel his loss so immediately and emotionally, not just intellectually as an experience I've spent so much time dissecting and crystalizing on the page. Relieved that I haven't turned him so completely into a story that I've removed the man, the loss, the part of me that will always be a little girl who misses her father.

But it wasn't his loss I felt that day—it was his presence that overwhelmed me, standing in the studio of one of his favorite artists of all time. Rembrandt's house was so full of Papa that I could almost hear him whispering, "Wow!" over my shoulder.

We walked up to the second floor and into the "curiosities" room. There were animal skulls of all sizes, massive art books with ornate leather covers, marble busts of Greek rulers, a whole shelf of interesting seashells, jars of large feathers, and a taxidermy armadillo. I laughed, delighted to see the great master's collecting habits so similar to my father's. I imagined him in the room with me and how ecstatic he would have been, his eyebrows raised in excitement as he leaned in and pointed out each and every cool thing. I wondered if Papa knew that Rembrandt was a collector like him, imagined writing him a postcard to describe this room and how just hearing about it from me would have thrilled him so thoroughly.

Next was the studio, where Rembrandt had set up his easel in the biggest room in the house, with the best light. I knew that if my father were there with me, all the giddiness of the curiosities room would have quieted into awe as we approached the easel where some of his favorite paintings had been made. I approached it with the hushed deference I knew my father would have had. And as I looked around and saw the full-but-organized shelves of brushes and paints and pallets smeared and caked with color, and smelled that earthy-but-chemical art studio smell, I could feel my father there with me so strongly it tingled on my skin like the heat of a New York summer day. And before I knew what was happening, tears were streaming down my face, my hands shaking, as tourists politely avoided me on their circuits around the room.

I realized then that I had succeeded in my spell: I had conjured my father. Before we left, I signed "Schactman" in the guest book, for us both.

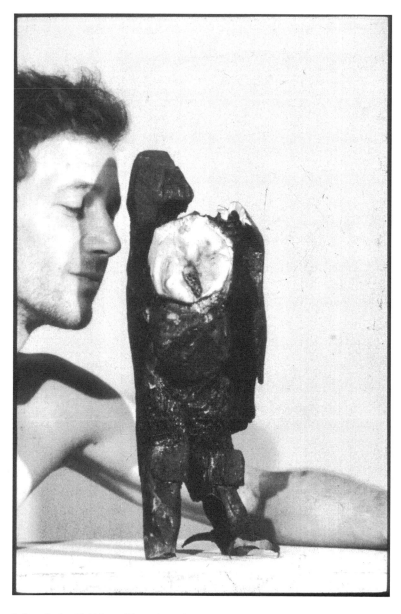

Self-portrait with Tylluan (From the artist's slides)

Top: Joe working, San Francisco, CA; approx. 1997

Bottom: Lilly drawing, Brooklyn, NY; approx. 1992

Heidi and Lilly in the backyard, San Francisco, CA; approx. 1995

Top: Joe, Heidi, and Lilly, the day Lilly was born, Buffalo, NY; 1988
Bottom: Wedding Day, New York, NY 1989

Top: Joe and Lilly taking a walk near the Loft, Brooklyn, NY; approx. 1989

Bottom: Lilly and Catman on the stoop, Brooklyn, NY; 1990

Top: Joe, Heidi, and Lilly at MoMA, New York, NY; 1989

Bottom: Joe and Lilly at a bar, New York, NY; approx. 1991

Top: Lilly and Heidi, San Francisco, CA; approx. 1994

Bottom: Joe and Lilly, San Francisco, CA; approx. 1996

Lilly and Joe laughing, the last time they saw each other,
San Francisco, CA; Easter Sunday, 2000

Acknowledgements

I owe a huge debt of gratitude to everyone who shared what they remember of my father with me, the good and the bad—whether those interviews ended up in the finished book or not. Thank you.

Especially my mother, who shared so much of herself in the process. This book is yours, too. I love you.

And to my husband Soomin, who let me talk through the challenges of this book with him for years, and comforted me when I cried in frustration over it, even when I wouldn't let him read a word. My coven of beloved sisters, Leah, Carly, Liz, and Courtney, for everything, always and forever. My writers' group, who have become the nexus of my writing community and an absolute lifeline over the last four years—Nina St. Pierre, Jeanna Kadlec, Deena ElGenaidi, and Angela Chen.

And to the friends and family who provided financial support when I launched a Kickstarter for this project nine years ago, estimating that I was a year away from finished. (Thanks for waiting. Sorry.) And Anne and Tosso, in whose guest house large portions of this book were written.

And so, so many people who gave me feedback and advice along the way, including but not limited to: Mark Greif, in whose research nonfiction class at the New School the first seeds of this project were planted; Wendy Walters, who was my adviser as I cobbled together the first feeble draft as my senior thesis; Ken Selden, who read several drafts as I banged my head against a wall and tried to figure out how to make this more than an inventory of my father's life; Brendan Spiegel, who published the first excerpts from early drafts at Narratively, and generously and carefully gave me feedback on the full manuscript; Julie Buntin, for encouraging me to cancel a bad book deal, which left the door open for this one; Lidia Yuknavitch, whose workshop cracked open something essential about what I was trying to do here; Melissa Febos, who sat at a cafeteria table at the Tin House Summer Workshop with me and told me that yes, there really was something here—and handed me a roadmap for the revision that finally turned this book into a book.

And of course, the team at SFWP for taking this book on after it was rejected over 50 times, for believing in this project and in me—especially Andrew Gifford, for sending me the acceptance email I had started to believe might never come; and Kate Anderson, for being the partner in crime every author hopes their editor will be. And Carmen Maria Machado for selecting this book as a winner of the SFWP Literary Award—validation from an icon like Carmen was enough of a boost to cancel out the years of rejection.

And while I'm at it, thank you to all of the agents and editors who rejected previous versions of this book over the years—you were right, it wasn't ready yet.

About the Author

Lilly Dancyger is a contributing editor at *Catapult*, and assistant editor at Barrelhouse Books. She's the editor of *Burn It Down*, a critically acclaimed anthology of essays on women's anger, and her writing has been published by *Rolling Stone*, *The Washington Post*, *The Atlantic*, *Playboy*, *Glamour*, *Longreads*, *The Rumpus*, and more. She lives in New York City.

Find her at lillydancyger.com and on Twitter: @lillydancyger

Other Memoirs from SFWP

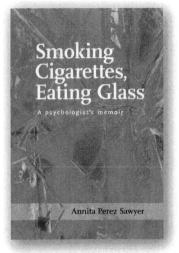

Smoking Cigarettes, Eating Glass
by Annita Perez Sawyer
A cautionary and fiercely honest story of careless psychiatric diagnosis, treatment, and resilience

Patagonian Road *by Kate McCahill*
A young woman's inspiring solo journey of discovery from Guatemala to Argentina

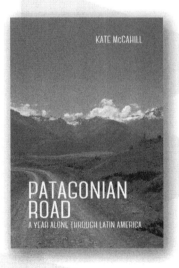
